T0196106

An Analysis of

Charles P. Kindleberger's

Manias, Panics, and Crashes: A History of Financial Crises

Nick Burton

Published by Macat International Ltd
24:13 Coda Centre, 189 Munster Road, London SW6 6AW.

Distributed exclusively by Routledge
2 Park Square, Milton Park, Abingdon, Oxon OX14 4RN
711 Third Avenue, New York, NY 10017, USA

Routledge is an imprint of the Taylor & Francis Group, an informa business

www.macat.com
info@macat.com

Cataloguing in Publication Data
A catalogue record for this book is available from the British Library.
Library of Congress Cataloguing-in-Publication Data is available upon request.
Cover illustration: Etienne Gilfillan

ISBN 978-1-912302-26-0 (hardback)
ISBN 978-1-912128-05-1 (paperback)
ISBN 978-1-912281-14-5 (e-book)

Notice
The information in this book is designed to orientate readers of the work under analysis,
to elucidate and contextualise its key ideas and themes, and to aid in the development
of critical thinking skills. It is not meant to be used, nor should it be used, as a
substitute for original thinking or in place of original writing or research. References and
notes are provided for informational purposes and their presence does not constitute
endorsement of the information or opinions therein. This book is presented solely for
educational purposes. It is sold on the understanding that the publisher is not engaged
to provide any scholarly advice. The publisher has made every effort to ensure that
this book is accurate and up-to-date, but makes no warranties or representations with
regard to the completeness or reliability of the information it contains. The information
and the opinions provided herein are not guaranteed or warranted to produce particular
results and may not be suitable for students of every ability. The publisher shall not be
liable for any loss, damage or disruption arising from any errors or omissions, or from
the use of this book, including, but not limited to, special, incidental, consequential or
other damages caused, or alleged to have been caused, directly or indirectly, by the
information contained within.

CONTENTS

THE MACAT LIBRARY

The Macat Library is a series of unique academic explorations of seminal works in the humanities and social sciences – books and papers that have had a significant and widely recognised impact on their disciplines. It has been created to serve as much more than just a summary of what lies between the covers of a great book. It illuminates and explores the influences on, ideas of, and impact of that book. Our goal is to offer a learning resource that encourages critical thinking and fosters a better, deeper understanding of important ideas.

Each publication is divided into three Sections: Influences, Ideas, and Impact. Each Section has four Modules. These explore every important facet of the work, and the responses to it.

This Section-Module structure makes a Macat Library book easy to use, but it has another important feature. Because each Macat book is written to the same format, it is possible (and encouraged!) to cross-reference multiple Macat books along the same lines of inquiry or research. This allows the reader to open up interesting interdisciplinary pathways.

To further aid your reading, lists of glossary terms and people mentioned are included at the end of this book (these are indicated by an asterisk [*] throughout) – as well as a list of works cited.

Macat has worked with the University of Cambridge to identify the elements of critical thinking and understand the ways in which six different skills combine to enable effective thinking.
Three allow us to fully understand a problem; three more give us the tools to solve it. Together, these six skills make up the **PACIER** model of critical thinking. They are:

ANALYSIS – understanding how an argument is built
EVALUATION – exploring the strengths and weaknesses of an argument
INTERPRETATION – understanding issues of meaning

CREATIVE THINKING – coming up with new ideas and fresh connections
PROBLEM-SOLVING – producing strong solutions
REASONING – creating strong arguments

To find out more, visit **WWW.MACAT.COM.**

CRITICAL THINKING AND
MANIAS, PANICS AND CRASHES

Primary critical thinking skill: EVALUATION
Secondary critical thinking skill: REASONING

Perhaps the most peculiar feature of a financial bubble – one that Charles Kindleberger's classic work *Manias, Panics and Crashes* draws particular attention to – is the inability of those trapped inside it to grasp the seriousness of their predicament. They know in principle that bubbles exist, and they know that the financial crashes that result from them are capable of destroying individuals' wealth and entire economies. Yet whenever and wherever a bubble begins to form, we're told that this time things are different, that there are sound reasons to continue to invest and to presume that prices will continue to rise steadily forever.

Kindleberger's achievement is to use the critical thinking skill of evaluation to examine this strange mindset and the arguments advanced in support of it. He harshly judges the acceptability of the reasons used to create such arguments, and highlights the issues of relevance and adequacy that give us every reason to doubt them. Kindleberger also uses his powers of reasoning to effect an unusual achievement – writing a work soundly rooted in economics that nonetheless engages and convinces a non-specialist audience of the correctness of his arguments.

ABOUT THE AUTHOR OF THE ORIGINAL WORK

Charles P. Kindleberger was born in New York City in 1910. He studied economics during the Great Depression of the 1930s, which followed a dramatic financial crash and was a time of unprecedented hardship—particularly in America. Kindleberger fought in World War II, and helped draft the Marshall Plan, an economic strategy that saw the US financially support the postwar rebuilding of Europe. These experiences shaped his career and thinking, as he tried to understand the real reasons for financial crises; they also exposed the crucial connections between national economies in a globalized world. When he died in 2003 at the age of 92, Kindleberger was hailed as a major figure in the world of economics.

ABOUT THE AUTHOR OF THE ANALYSIS

Dr Nicholas Burton holds degrees in both economics and literature. He currently lectures in Oxford and London.

ABOUT MACAT

GREAT WORKS FOR CRITICAL THINKING

Macat is focused on making the ideas of the world's great thinkers accessible and comprehensible to everybody, everywhere, in ways that promote the development of enhanced critical thinking skills.

It works with leading academics from the world's top universities to produce new analyses that focus on the ideas and the impact of the most influential works ever written across a wide variety of academic disciplines. Each of the works that sit at the heart of its growing library is an enduring example of great thinking. But by setting them in context – and looking at the influences that shaped their authors, as well as the responses they provoked – Macat encourages readers to look at these classics and game-changers with fresh eyes. Readers learn to think, engage and challenge their ideas, rather than simply accepting them.

'Macat offers an amazing first-of-its-kind tool for interdisciplinary learning and research. Its focus on works that transformed their disciplines and its rigorous approach, drawing on the world's leading experts and educational institutions, opens up a world-class education to anyone.'

Andreas Schleicher,
Director for Education and Skills, Organisation for Economic Co-operation and Development

'Macat is taking on some of the major challenges in university education … They have drawn together a strong team of active academics who are producing teaching materials that are novel in the breadth of their approach.'

Prof Lord Broers,
former Vice-Chancellor of the University of Cambridge

'The Macat vision is exceptionally exciting. It focuses upon new modes of learning which analyse and explain seminal texts which have profoundly influenced world thinking and so social and economic development. It promotes the kind of critical thinking which is essential for any society and economy. This is the learning of the future.'

Rt Hon Charles Clarke, former UK Secretary of State for Education

'The Macat analyses provide immediate access to the critical conversation surrounding the books that have shaped their respective discipline, which will make them an invaluable resource to all of those, students and teachers, working in the field.'

Professor William Tronzo, University of California at San Diego

WAYS IN TO THE TEXT

KEY POINTS

- Charles Poor Kindleberger was an American economist. He was born in 1910, and died in 2003 at the age of 92.
- His book *Manias, Panics, and Crashes* (1978) analyzes the nature of financial crises,* past and present.
- *Manias, Panics and Crashes* argues that markets are inherently unstable because of irrational behavior combined with surges in the availability of credit.

Who Is Charles P. Kindleberger?

Charles Poor Kindleberger, author of *Manias, Panics, and Crashes: A History of Financial Crises* (1978), was born in New York City in 1910. During his career as a distinguished economist and academic, he went against conventional wisdom in the 1970s, arguing that the world's financial markets were not as ordered and efficient* as people thought. Kindleberger asserted that markets are unstable, prone to crisis, and at times in need of radical intervention.

Kindleberger's career started with economics* degrees from the University of Pennsylvania and Columbia University, where he earned his doctorate. Before and after World War II* (1939–45) he worked for the US government and helped to draft the Marshall Plan.* This supported the rebuilding of Europe, where infrastructure and industry had been badly damaged in the course of the war. He joined the economics faculty of the Massachusetts Institute of Technology (MIT) in 1948.

In his economic thinking, Kindleberger pursued an international perspective; he was one of the first thinkers to conceive of the economies of individual nations as interdependent. In the 1970s, he noticed certain changes in the international economy that he thought were likely to encourage volatility (that is, instability) and financial crises. The patterns he observed in how economic crises develop laid the foundation for his most influential ideas.

Kindleberger had a vast knowledge of economic history and wrote using a literary, narrative style totally at odds with the more mathematical analyses of his peers. *Manias, Panics, and Crashes* articulates the inherent instability of the global economy that was being reawoken in the 1970s. In this sense, his book proved prophetic, predicting many of the twenty-first-century financial meltdowns such as the financial crisis of 2008.*

What Does *Manias, Panics, and Crashes* Say?

Manias, Panics, and Crashes is a classic work of economic history, surveying a vast number of past financial crises. These examples serve Kindleberger's theoretical argument: that each financial crisis is *not* unique. Throughout history, such crises have had much in common. These consistent features and stages of development are what Kindleberger calls a "biologic regularity"* that can be decoded through an examination of economic history.[1] Once this is understood, economic policy can be designed to minimize the damage caused by such chaos.

Kindleberger's argument in *Manias, Panics, and Crashes* rejects the models of economic efficiency that were popular in the 1970s. These theories relied on the idea that investors*—those who provide capital in the hope of profiting from the investment later—act rationally. Instead, Kindleberger saw financial crises as the product of mob psychology among these market players. The wild optimism of a "mania" is typically fed by a surge in the supply of credit, and Kindleberger pinpointed this as a core issue. Easy access to credit enables investors to purchase assets* through debt. During the overoptimistic "mania" of rising prices, such investors get into vast amounts of debt—while assuming that the prices of their assets will continue to rise forever.

When the prices of such assets stop rising (as they inevitably must), a sudden "panic" sets in, leading to a "crash" in asset values. Banks and other financial institutions are liable to go bust as loans are not repaid, and they themselves can be heavily indebted. A wave of insolvency can then develop, and spread to several countries at once through international contagion.* For example, if investors borrow a great deal of money from Mexican banks that they cannot pay back, the banks in Mexico are likely to go bust. American banks might have a lot of money invested in Mexican banks that can no longer be paid back, and suddenly find themselves insolvent as well. British banks might have no investments in Mexico at all, but have huge amounts of money in American banks. So the Mexican crisis could end up bankrupting British banks as a knock-on effect. To make this point, Kindleberger quotes the nineteenth-century economist Alfred Marshall* who said, "The evils of reckless trading are always apt to spread beyond the persons immediately concerned."[2] This is a principal reason for the world's economy being so fragile.

In *Manias, Panics, and Crashes* Kindleberger argues that you cannot stop such crises; you can only contain them. He believed that a single country needed to take charge of the global economy and stabilize it in periods of turbulence. In the aftermath of World War I* (1914–18), when Britain faded as a global power, he thought the United States should take over this role.

Why Does *Manias, Panics, and Crashes* Matter?

Manias, Panics and Crashes is a famous, incisive analysis of how financial crises work. It first appeared in 1978, when the world was entering a new period of global economic fragility. Over the next 40 years, six of the ten biggest booms and busts in the history of capitalism* (the economic and social system dominant in the West, and increasingly throughout the world, in which business is conducted for private profit) would take place. The sustained popularity of Kindleberger's book shows that international financial crises continue to be a primary issue for the world economy. Since Kindleberger's death in 2003, the economist Robert Z. Aliber* has edited and updated subsequent editions of *Manias, Panics, and Crashes*.

But Kindleberger's text is not just extraordinarily timely. Moving through the long history of financial crises, he creates an entertaining text that still communicates a serious point about the inherent instability of markets. He argues that this volatility will never disappear but can only be managed. The irrational behavior of investors is a constant across time and is still prevalent today.

In 1978, conventional wisdom among economists was based on the assumption that self-interested market participants like bankers and investors make rational choices. Kindleberger insisted on the constant presence of irrational investing behavior—an unorthodox position in 1978. Since then, entire new fields of economic study have emerged to explore irrational investment decisions—particularly the field of behavioral economics*—and to incorporate psychology* into economic models. These areas have produced Nobel Prize* winners, including Robert J. Shiller,* one of Kindleberger's former students, who described him as having "a great influence on [his] thinking."[3]

Outside academia, Kindleberger's book has also influenced politicians and policymakers, some of whom have had to manage worldwide financial crises. *Manias, Panics, and Crashes* is now essential reading for anyone interested in understanding the market cycle of boom and bust.* The work is also innovative in its style. Kindleberger's literary, narrative voice differs from the mathematics and models often found in economic texts. This makes *Manias, Panics, and Crashes* an engaging read, and a human story.

NOTES

1   Charles P. Kindleberger and Robert Z. Aliber, *Manias, Panics, and Crashes: A History of Financial Crises* (Basingstoke: Palgrave MacMillan, 2015), 20.

2   Kindleberger and Aliber, *Manias, Panics, and Crashes*, 56.

3   Robert J. Shiller, *Irrational Exuberance* (Princeton: Princeton University Press, 2015), 92.

SECTION 1
INFLUENCES

MODULE 1
THE AUTHOR AND THE
HISTORICAL CONTEXT

KEY POINTS

* *Manias, Panics, and Crashes: A History of Financial Crises* presents a wide-ranging history of financial crises,* and a convincing theory as to why they occur.

* Kindleberger's academic education was enhanced by his work in the US government before and after World War II* (1939–45).

* The 1970s reignited turbulence in the world economy that deeply concerned Kindleberger, giving urgency to the ideas in his book.

Why Read this Text?

Charles P. Kindleberger's *Manias, Panics and Crashes: A History of Financial Crises* was first published in 1978 and is now in its seventh edition. It has become a classic of economic* history and is still frequently cited in the worlds of academia, finance, politics, and journalism.

The book describes a panoramic history of financial crises going back to the birth of commerce itself. Kindleberger describes in detail the stages such financial crises have had in common. In doing so, he asserts that not all crises are unique—they actually share a "biologic regularity"* that reflects an inherent tendency in the markets to boom and bust,* a cycle that repeats itself in particular stages.[1] In the first phase, an external shock or "displacement"* occurs that leads to economic expansion; business firms become "euphorically" optimistic and investment surges because credit is easy to obtain.[2] The prices of

> ❝ The three decades since the early 1980s have been the most tumultuous in monetary history in terms of the number, scope, and severity of banking crises. ❞
>
> Charles P. Kindleberger, *Manias, Panics and Crashes: A History of Financial Crises*

securities* (financial agreements concerning ownership such as stocks, bonds, and options) and real estate rise dramatically until another shock—perhaps a change in government policy—leads to a pause in the pace of these price increases, which in turn triggers a crash: "There is no plateau, no 'middle ground' … the rush to sell these securities becomes self-fulfilling and so precipitous that it resembles a panic."[3]

While his dissection of financial crises was not entirely original, Kindleberger was among the first to place such events in an international context. This offered fresh insight that is increasingly relevant to today's global economy. As the US economist Robert M. Solow* says in his introduction to the seventh edition, "Any reader of this book will come away with the distinct notion that larger quantities of liquid capital sloshing around the world should raise the possibility that they will overflow the container."[4] Kindleberger's argument offers potential solutions to slow down or minimize (if not eliminate) such financial crises, and forms a key contribution to this urgent issue in today's political economy.

Author's Life

Charles Kindleberger was born in 1910. He graduated from the University of Pennsylvania in 1932 and received a doctorate in economics from Columbia University in 1937, studying under the monetary* theorist James W. Angell.* It is notable that Kindleberger's undergraduate education took place during the Great Depression,* a period of unprecedented financial chaos that began in the late 1920s.

After serving in the military during World War II, Kindleberger became chief of the State Department's Division of German and Austrian Economic Affairs from 1945 to 1947, and advisor to the European Recovery Program from 1947 to 1948. While holding the latter post, he helped design and implement the Marshall Plan,* a massive American effort to revive the European economy after the war. These roles added practical policy experience to Kindleberger's academic learning, and it has been argued that they helped form the ideas described in *Manias, Panics, and Crashes*—particularly his ideas on which countries and international institutions might stabilize the global economy.[5]

In 1948 Kindleberger began an academic career in economics at the Massachusetts Institute of Technology, where he retired as a chaired professor in 1976. He worked as a consultant to the US government many times over this span, and published a great many books and articles. His evolving focus on the international dimensions of financial crises culminated in two texts that are now considered classics: *The World In Depression, 1929–1939* (first published in 1973) and *Manias, Panics, and Crashes* (1978).

Author's Background

Kindleberger trained as an economist during the Great Depression. Within his academic subject, a fierce debate would rage for decades over what exactly had caused this economic catastrophe. Revered economists proposed their own (very different) theories. The British economist John Maynard Keynes,* for example, said the problem had been a chronic lack of consumer demand, which should have been propped up by government spending. The US economist Milton Friedman* argued that it had been the failure of the US Federal Reserve* (the central bank of the United States) to provide banks with additional funds to meet the demands of depositors. Decades later, Kindleberger would also be drawn to this prominent subject, offering a more international analysis. After World War I* (1914–18), he argued, Great Britain's role as leader of the international economy was fading, just when it was needed most; America, meanwhile, was reluctant to take on the task. The resulting vacuum allowed the world to sink into the Depression.

Kindleberger worked for the US government during its reconstruction of the world economy after World War II. During the 1950s and 1960s, he witnessed (relative) global economic stability— but fundamental changes then took place that greatly concerned him. The international economy of the early 1970s was remarkably volatile, with huge changes in the day-to-day and month-to-month prices of commodities (exchangeable goods), currencies, bonds, stocks* (tradable shares in a business) and real estate, relative to their long-run averages.[6] New technology was clearly playing a role in this: innovations in communications and computing meant that money could travel around the world much more actively, with investors* shifting funds to a foreign center for even a "small anticipated incremental return."[7] These quick movements in capital* only encourage bubbles,* a "bubble" being when the price of an asset* (property) or security* (a financial agreement signifying ownership in a public-traded corporation) increases significantly in a way that cannot be explained by economic fundamentals.[8]

Kindleberger perceived a new global instability reminiscent of the era leading up to the Great Depression, and began to study it in terms of historical precedents. The result was *Manias, Panics, and Crashes*.

NOTES

1   Charles P. Kindleberger and Robert Z. Aliber, *Manias, Panics, and Crashes: A History of Financial Crises* (Basingstoke: Palgrave MacMillan, 2015), 20.

2   Kindleberger and Aliber, *Manias, Panics, and Crashes*, 104.

3   Kindleberger and Aliber, *Manias, Panics, and Crashes*, 20.

4   Kindleberger and Aliber, *Manias, Panics, and Crashes*, viii.

5   Stephen Meardon, "On Kindleberger and Hegemony: From Berlin to M.I.T. and Back," Bowdoin Digital Commons, September 29, 2013, accessed March 22, 2016, http://digitalcommons.bowdoin.edu/cgi/viewcontent.cgi?article=1003&context=econpapers.

6   Kindleberger and Aliber, *Manias, Panics, and Crashes*, 5.

7   Kindleberger and Aliber, *Manias, Panics, and Crashes*, 25.

8   Kindleberger and Aliber, *Manias, Panics, and Crashes*, 43.

MODULE 2
ACADEMIC CONTEXT

KEY POINTS

- When Kindleberger wrote *Manias, Panics, and Crashes*, economics* departments were largely in thrall to ideas of rational behavior and efficient* outcomes (that is, the idea that an asset's* price is an accurate indication of its value).

- For adherents of the efficient market hypothesis,* international trade promotes efficiency, and any turbulence is part of that process.

- Kindleberger rejected this premise, instead focusing on the irrational elements of international investment that promote instability.

The Work In Its Context

Charles P. Kindleberger wrote the first edition of *Manias, Panics, and Crashes: A History of Financial Crises* in the 1970s. At that time, most economists who studied financial markets were persuaded by the efficient market hypothesis (EMH), which in its purest form rules out the possibility of bubbles*—economically hazardous overpricing—in asset prices (in real estate or securities,* for example).[1]

They had a logical reason for doing so. Led by economists like the Nobel Prize–winner E. F. Fama* and the famous Princeton professor Burton G. Malkiel,* adherents of the EMH asserted that security prices capture all available news and information about their respective companies. If a share price does not do this, these shares have been priced incorrectly, and people will flock to exploit this imbalance (by either buying or selling the incorrectly priced stock),* causing the inefficiency to disappear rapidly. So making significant amounts of

> **❝** The loss of connection with rationality reflects that the investors, lenders, borrowers, and the bank and financial regulators fail to recognize that a crash is always the end game for the mania. **❞**
>
> Charles P. Kindleberger, *Manias, Panics, and Crashes: A History of Financial Crises*

money from exploiting these inefficiencies is more or less impossible. The same logic ruled out the possibility of financial bubbles; EMH theory blamed past bubbles on undeveloped, fraud-prone markets, and asserted that such bubbles are unlikely to occur in sophisticated, well-regulated modern markets.[2] Kindleberger argues the opposite in *Manias, Panics, and Crashes,* saying that completely irrational behavior often drives markets and creates crises.

Kindleberger was also one of the few economists of his generation to be skeptical of "monetarists"* like Milton Friedman,* who held sway in the 1950s and 1960s.[3] A monetarist is an economist who believes that the performance of an economy is primarily driven by changes in the supply of money. For monetarists, bubbles can be controlled if the supply of money becomes more restricted—through a rise in interest rates, for example. Kindleberger instead argued that many of the booms in real estate or stock prices occur because of surges in the supply of credit and the inflow of international investment.[4]

Overview of the Field

Kindleberger's study reveals a long history of prominent thinkers who have engaged with the subject of financial crises, and how governments or central banks might be able to contain them. He describes a rich tapestry of contemporary and historic events, all centered upon various surges in prices of securities and real estate, and the subsequent crashes caused by them.[5] Kindleberger frequently quotes "classical economists"* (a group of economists from the eighteenth and nineteenth centuries who theorized about market economies). This group included figures like the economist and philosopher John Stuart Mill* and the economist Walter Bagehot,* both British, who expounded concepts of market instability that Kindleberger would develop.[6]

For example, it was Mill who first raised the question as to how much credit households, firms, and governments can command at a given time.[7] This question is central to Kindleberger's investigation. He also consistently cites the "Bagehot doctrine,"* arguing that central banks must provide an unlimited amount of credit to solvent banks during a crisis, at a penalty interest rate (this "penalty" ensuring that the central bank will truly be used as the "lender of last resort.")*[8] Kindleberger pushes this idea further, arguing that such help must also include insolvent banks (banks that cannot return cash invested by their customers).[9]

Kindleberger was writing at a time when the efficient market hypothesis was at the height of its popularity. In his eyes, at the heart of this theory is the assumption of "rational expectations": that investors react to changes in economic variables as if they are always fully aware of the long-term implications of each of these changes.[10] For Kindleberger, this idea is utterly discredited by history: "Rationality is an a priori assumption about the way the world should work rather than a description of the way the world has actually worked."[11]

Academic Influences

While the efficient market hypothesis was widely popular in the 1970s, the economist Hyman Minsky's* "financial instability hypothesis"* (developed in the 1960s) was remarkably out of fashion. This is understandable, as he essentially argued the opposite case: that the financial system in a market economy is inherently unstable, fragile, and prone to crisis.[12] Minsky supported this view with a theory of credit cycles that is perhaps the primary influence on Kindleberger's book. Essentially, Minsky believed that supplies of credit are procyclical:* that is, increases in the supply of credit prolong the expansion of the boom, and decreases in the supply of credit intensify the subsequent crash.[13] The "Minsky model"* is an extremely useful tool for explaining financial crises,* past and present, as so many of them follow a surge in real estate prices that stems from an increase in the supply of credit.[14]

Minsky's model follows in the tradition of the same classical economists who so interested Kindleberger,[15] in particular, the "classical" ideas of market instability; these earlier economists used terms like "overtrading" to describe a mania, and said that it leads to a "revulsion" period (panic) and ultimately "discredit" (a crash). They also concentrated on the variability in the supply of credit, a focus amplified by Minsky. Kindleberger can be seen as a more recent member of this intellectual school of thought, adapting an existing tradition to a more international context.

NOTES

1 *Economist*, "Of Manias, Panics, and Crashes," July 19, 2003, accessed March 22, 2016, http://www.economist.com/node/1923462.

2 *Economist*, "Of Manias, Panics, and Crashes."

3 Charles P. Kindleberger and Robert Z. Aliber, *Manias, Panics, and Crashes: A History of Financial Crises* (Basingstoke: Palgrave MacMillan, 2015), 2.

4 Kindleberger and Aliber, *Manias, Panics and Crashes,* 25.

5 Kindleberger and Aliber, *Manias, Panics, and Crashes*, 25.

6 Kindleberger and Aliber, *Manias, Panics, and Crashes*, 27.

7 Kindleberger and Aliber, *Manias, Panics, and Crashes*, 85.

8 Kindleberger and Aliber, *Manias, Panics, and Crashes*, 278.

9 Kindleberger and Aliber, *Manias, Panics, and Crashes*, 323.

10 Kindleberger and Aliber, *Manias, Panics, and Crashes*, 53.

11 Kindleberger and Aliber, *Manias, Panics, and Crashes*, 55.

12 Kindleberger and Aliber, *Manias, Panics, and Crashes*, 27.

13 Kindleberger and Aliber, *Manias, Panics, and Crashes*, 2.

14 Kindleberger and Aliber, *Manias, Panics, and Crashes*, 27.

15 Kindleberger and Aliber, *Manias, Panics, and Crashes*, 39.

MODULE 3
THE PROBLEM

KEY POINTS

- The main question engaging Kindleberger's academic peers in the mid-1970s was how markets promote efficient* outcomes.

- Many economists debated the reasons for the catastrophic economic downturn of the late 1920s and 1930s, the Great Depression,* and followed the "demand-driven" theory of the English economist John Maynard Keynes* (according to which a faltering economy can be stimulated by government spending), or the money-supply theory of the US economist Milton Friedman* (according to which an economy can be stabilized through controls of the amount of money in circulation).

- Kindleberger took a more international perspective on the Great Depression, and thought that recent developments in the world economy foster even greater instability.

Core Question

The core questions that Charles P. Kindleberger seeks to answer in *Manias, Panics, and Crashes: A History of Financial Crises* are: Why do financial crises* happen? Why do they now seem to be growing bigger and more common? And what can be done about them? "If many financial crises have a stylized form," he asks, "should there be a standard policy response?"[1]

Kindleberger saw that most bubbles*—past and present—are fed by a surge in the supply of credit, but there was also a new source of global fragility that was unique to his age. Global "payment imbalances"* developed in the late 1960s, and continued through the

> 66 Nevertheless despite the lack of perfect comparability across periods, the conclusion is unmistakable that banking crises have been more extensive and pervasive. 99
>
> Charles P. Kindleberger, *Manias, Panics, and Crashes: A History of Financial Crises*

next several decades.[2] To explain what a payment imbalance is, we might consider the case of Saudi Arabia.

In the 1970s, many of the world's top oil-producing nations agreed to purposefully decrease the production of crude oil—a move that drove up international oil prices, greatly enhancing the profit margins for oil producers. The oil-producing nation Saudi Arabia was exporting far more to other countries than it was importing, which created a large "payment imbalance" between it and the nations importing its oil. The huge surplus wealth that Saudi Arabia gained from trading with these countries could then be invested globally to earn further returns, in whatever assets* the Saudis preferred—they could invest in Thai securities* (tradable assets such as stocks)* one day, helping to drive up the price in that market, before suddenly selling them and reinvesting the proceeds in Brazilian securities—or any other worldwide investment that appealed at that moment.

So, this wandering money travels around the world in search of higher profits as a "cross-border investment flow"* (financial arrangements that cross national borders, typically taking the form of loans, acquisitions, or credit). There are big currency issues in cross-border investment flows.[3] If money from around the world rushes into the Brazilian stock market, the value of the Brazilian currency itself will also rise. If Brazilian securities peak and no longer earn large returns, all those global investors* may sell at once—so the price of Brazilian securities *and* the price of the currency will crash as investors suddenly run for the exits, trying to sell their assets before their inevitable and rapid depreciation (loss in value). Thus, such investment flows can leave a country with both a financial *and* a currency crisis.*⁴

The Participants

For adherents of the efficient market hypothesis* (the idea that asset prices, including stock prices, capture all available information about that asset)—so popular in economics* departments during the 1970s—these cross-border investment flows reflect global efficiency in the long term. Global money, they would argue, is following good, and perhaps underpriced, investments worldwide, and so raising their price to an efficient equilibrium while lowering the price of less worthy investments ("equilibrium" here refers to the idea that the prices of assets settle to reflect their true, balanced, value). It may be a bumpy ride, but stability can be achieved just by letting international markets function, unhampered by regulation.

Monetarists* like Milton Friedman* (those who believe that a market's performance is closely associated with the amount of money in circulation in an economy) admit that markets can get dangerously overheated, and see interest rates*—the price of borrowing—as a means of creating stability. If a government can control the domestic supply of money by raising interest rates, for example, it can restrain overinflated markets: the higher interest raises the price of borrowing money, so fewer people will do so. Ultimately this lowers demand across an economy. As Kindleberger puts it, "Many monetarists insist that many, perhaps most, of the cyclical difficulties of the past have resulted from mismanagement of the monetary mechanism."⁵

A string of financial crises over the past few decades has turned up the volume of this debate, with many more voices joining in. The economist Robert Z. Aliber*—who took over the role of editing and updating *Manias, Panics, and Crashes* after Kindleberger's death—notes in the seventh edition, the 2008 global financial crisis* and the ensuing recession has inspired a spate of books on the topic. They tend to be written by three types of authors: journalists, academics, and "insiders" who have worked in finance.[6] Overall, Aliber is less than impressed: "The shortcoming of most of these books is that they give no explanation for why the crisis occurred when it did, nor do they have an explanation for why some countries were involved but not others."[7]

The Contemporary Debate

In stark contrast to the popular theories of his contemporaries, Kindleberger came to a very different view of the nature of financial crises. Drawing on the economist Hyman Minksy's* relatively unpopular financial instability hypothesis,* according to which economic prosperity leads to reckless investment behavior, Kindleberger developed Minsky's argument that the reckless use of a credit cycle leads to a mania, panic, and an inevitable crash.

A wave of global financial crises commenced soon after the first publication of *Manias, Panics, and Crashes,* at a time when the authority of the efficient market hypothesis was already starting to dwindle. For example, Daniel Kahneman* and Amos Tversky*—researchers in the field of the human mind and economic behavior—published a study on "behavioral decision theory" in 1979, claiming that investors are systematically overconfident in their capacity to predict future stock prices and corporate earnings.[8] Their conclusion anticipates the emergence of behavioral finance,* a field that turns to the discipline of psychology* to answer questions about economic behavior, and which has come to seriously challenge the efficiency market hypothesis, while also supporting Kindleberger's claims of irrational, "herd" behavior among investors.

That said, when *Manias, Panics, and Crashes* was first published in 1978, Friedman's monetarism was still convincing major policymakers. From 1979–82, the Federal Reserve* (the central bank of the United States) began to limit the growth of the money supply in the US economy in an effort to tame high inflation* (a fall in the value of money, and rise in the value of prices); this effort became known as the great "monetarist experiment," and had decidedly mixed results.[9] Nonetheless, monetary tools (basically, measures to control the supply of money in an economy) remained quite popular, and are still seen as a powerful way to tame the larger fluctuations of a boom-and-bust* business cycle.

Finally, in 1978 there were economists and prominent opinion-makers who claimed that increased regulation was the way to prevent financial crises—indeed, there are *always* people making this claim.[10] Kindleberger actually disagrees with this policy, asserting something that is almost heresy: that seeing financial institutions such as banks as responsible for a financial crisis is to mistake "the symptoms of the crisis for the causes."[11] In Kindleberger's view, even if these firms *were* responsible for the crash, banking "is difficult to regulate because new institutions develop that circumvent the regulations."[12]

NOTES

1   Charles P. Kindleberger and Robert Z. Aliber, *Manias, Panics, and Crashes: A History of Financial Crises*, (Basingstoke: Palgrave MacMillan, 2015), 235.

2   Kindleberger and Aliber, *Manias, Panics, and Crashes*, 219.

3   Kindleberger and Aliber, *Manias, Panics, and Crashes*, 220.

4   Kindleberger and Aliber, *Manias, Panics, and Crashes*, 222.

5   Kindleberger and Aliber, *Manias, Panics, and Crashes*, 28.

6   Kindleberger and Aliber, *Manias, Panics, and Crashes*, 16–17.

7   Kindleberger and Aliber, *Manias, Panics, and Crashes*, 17.

8   Burton G. Malkiel, "The Efficient Market Hypothesis and Its Critics," *Journal of Economic Perspectives* 17, no. 1 (Winter, 2003): 63.

9   David R. Hakes and David C. Rose, "The 1979–1982 Monetary Policy Experiment: Monetarist, Anti-Monetarist, or Quasi-Monetarist?" *Journal of Post Keynesian Economics*, 15, no. 2 (Winter, 1992–3): 281–8.

10 Kindleberger and Aliber, *Manias, Panics, and Crashes*, 239.
11 Kindleberger and Aliber, *Manias, Panics, and Crashes*, 3.
12 Kindleberger and Aliber, *Manias, Panics, and Crashes*, 28.

MODULE 4
THE AUTHOR'S CONTRIBUTION

KEY POINTS

- Kindleberger asserts that irrational investment behavior combined with a surge in the supply of credit creates financial crises,* which then spread internationally.

- Kindleberger's argument leans heavily on the economist Hyman Minsky's* "financial instability hypothesis,"* which sees financial crises arising from the increased availability of credit in times of economic prosperity.

- *Manias, Panics, and Crashes* broke new ground as the first book of its kind to examine financial meltdowns from an international perspective.

Author's Aims

The primary objective of Charles P. Kindleberger's *Manias, Panics, and Crashes: A History of Financial Crises* is to put the economic assumption of "rationality" on trial: "The central issue is whether the markets in securities* and real estate are always rational, or whether speculation can be destabilizing."[1] For Kindleberger, the idea that investors* always act "rationally" is clearly a myth, debunked by the pure weight of historical evidence. Those who believe otherwise, such as adherents of the efficient market hypothesis,* according to which the price of assets* on the financial markets eventually reflects their true value if the market is left to its own devices, are living in a fantasyland.[2]

Kindleberger aims to prove that the source of "manias" (a buying spree of financial products that drives up prices) is a surge in the supply of credit and cross-border investment flows* (a financial arrangement such as a loan or acquisition) during times of economic boom.[3] Inevitably, the tide turns and the price of securities and real estate

> 66 A general collapse of credit, however short the time it lasts, is more fearful than the most terrible earthquake. 99
> Michel Chevalier, *Lettres sur l'Amérique du Nord*

(driven by the easy availability of money through credit) begins to decline, provoking a "panic" and then a "crash."[4] Finally, Kindleberger shows that there are no easy solutions to this predicament, which has grown to global proportions.[5] He ultimately makes a case for a "lender of last resort"* on an international level—that is to say, a financial institution (or entire country) that can bail out banks around the world and so prevent the collapse of the global financial system.[6]

Part of Kindleberger's purpose is to unlock the relationship between the irrational behavior of investors and the institutions they use, as such behavior seems to depend so much on this.[7] For example, he notes that in times of economic "euphoria" it is not only investors who become overly optimistic, pointing out that "authorities recognize that something exceptional is happening and while they are mindful of earlier manias, 'this time it's different,' and they have extensive explanations for why it is different."[8] It was not very long ago, after all, that Gordon Brown,* then the United Kingdom's chancellor of the exchequer (chief of the ministry of finance) declared "an end to [the] boom and bust"* cycle.[9] The 2008 global financial crisis* proved how wrong this grand pronouncement was.

Approach
Kindleberger's approach has been compared to that of the influential English evolutionary theorist Charles Darwin,* in that he moves through the history of financial turmoil "collecting, examining, and classifying interesting specimens."[10] There is the sense that Kindleberger isn't just cherry-picking "specimens" that support a preconceived position, but instead forms an argument based on

historical evidence.[11] He ends up with a unique—and uniquely insightful—narrative that reveals underlying and unifying causes of financial crises.

A major cornerstone of Kindleberger's approach is to emphasize, as the economist Hyman Minsky did before him, that changes in the supply of credit are "pro-cyclical."*[12] This means that during periods of economic boom, credit becomes much more plentiful and easy to obtain as investors experience "euphoria" about future financial prospects.[13] The supply of credit is then sharply reduced when the euphoria begins to dissipate, and recession begins to set in (as in the American "credit crunch"* of 2007, when credit became difficult to obtain). This decrease in credit greatly intensifies the crash when it finally comes, often threatening the entire financial system with bankruptcy.[14] It is this perspective that leads Kindleberger to argue for an international "lender of last resort," which can provide the bailouts necessary to prevent total financial collapse.

Contribution in Context

It is common for people to criticize Kindleberger's argument as not wholly original.[15] The "Minsky model,"* which carefully argued that an economy's supply of credit is the primary source of booms and busts, existed well before Kindleberger's book. Kindleberger's originality was to extend this perspective to an international context, noting, for example, "that the failure of a bank in Ohio led to shortages of credit in Hamburg and Scandinavia."[16] Kindleberger wanted to reveal the international contagion* of financial crises, as "historically euphoria has often spread from one country to others," and, likewise, the resulting panics and crashes.[17] Another example of Kindleberger's global perspective was his keen awareness of international currency speculators,* who often sell off a country's currency as its boom turns to bust; this can augment a country's financial crisis with a currency crisis*—when a currency falls in value, discouraging potential investors (among other consequences).

In expanding on Minsky's ideas, Kindleberger also examined the stages of a financial crisis in much greater detail. First there is the "displacement,"* in which the removal of regulations of banking practices or investments leads to a boom, or a new technology or innovation radically improves profitability in a market (the boom in information technologies in the late 1990s following the invention of the Internet, for example, saw a surge of investment in Internet companies).[18] This typically leads to an increase in the price of such assets, creating a "euphoria" that draws more investors in.[19] A "mania" develops with super-high prices fuelled by speculation (investors seeking profits), until there is a significant event that signals the end of the boom: the failure of a bank or major firm, for example.[20] The "revulsion" phase then begins: there is a mass, panicked sell-off, and prices plummet.[21] This is a framework drawn from history, but Kindleberger explores it with an accuracy that was remarkably fresh when it first appeared. It has proved to resonate since with academics, financiers, and policymakers.

NOTES

1   Charles P. Kindleberger and Robert Z. Aliber, *Manias, Panics, and Crashes: A History of Financial Crises*, (Basingstoke: Palgrave MacMillan, 2015), 27.

2   Kindleberger and Aliber, *Manias, Panics, and Crashes*, 55.

3   Kindleberger and Aliber, *Manias, Panics, and Crashes*, 31, 78, 201.

4   Kindleberger and Aliber, *Manias, Panics, and Crashes*, 20.

5   Kindleberger and Aliber, *Manias, Panics, and Crashes*, 23.

6   Kindleberger and Aliber, *Manias, Panics, and Crashes*, 279.

7   Kindleberger and Aliber, *Manias, Panics, and Crashes*, vii.

8   Kindleberger and Aliber, *Manias, Panics, and Crashes*, 41.

9   James Kirkup, "Gordon Brown admits he was wrong to claim he had ended 'boom and bust,'" *Telegraph,* November 21, 2008, accessed March 22, 2016, http://www.telegraph.co.uk/finance/recession/3497533/Gordon-Brown-admits-he-was-wrong-to-claim-he-had-ended-boom-and-bust.html.

10 Kindleberger and Aliber, *Manias, Panics, and Crashes*, vii.

11 Kindleberger and Aliber, *Manias, Panics, and Crashes*, vii.

12 Kindleberger and Aliber, *Manias, Panics, and Crashes*, 1.

13 Kindleberger and Aliber, *Manias, Panics and Crashes*, 84, 104.

14 Kindleberger and Aliber, *Manias, Panics, and Crashes*, 1, 245.

15 *Economist*, "Of Manias, Panics, and Crashes," July 19, 2003, accessed March 22, 2015, http://www.economist.com/node/1923462.

16 Kindleberger and Aliber, *Manias, Panics, and Crashes*, 2.

17 Kindleberger and Aliber, *Manias, Panics, and Crashes*, 44.

18 Kindleberger and Aliber, *Manias, Panics, and Crashes*, 72.

19 Kindleberger and Aliber, *Manias, Panics, and Crashes*, 41.

20 Kindleberger and Aliber, *Manias, Panics, and Crashes*, 46.

21 Kindleberger and Aliber, *Manias, Panics, and Crashes*, 46.

SECTION 2
IDEAS

MODULE 5
MAIN IDEAS

KEY POINTS

- Kindleberger focuses his study on irrational behavior by investors,* surges in credit, cross-border investment flows,* and how investment manias quickly turn into panics and then crashes.

- Through a wealth of historical examples, Kindleberger theorizes that there is a "biologic regularity"* to financial crises,* showing that they share the same stages of development; he then suggests what measures can be taken to contain them.

- Kindleberger thought that the field of economics* had become too mathematical; he used a "literary economics" with a strong narrative to communicate his argument in human terms.

Key Themes

Charles P. Kindleberger's *Manias, Panics, and Crashes: A History of Financial Crises* identifies the common elements that lead to major economic breakdowns: irrational behavior by investors, surges in credit, cross-border investment flows, and investment manias that quickly turn into panics and then crashes. Kindleberger finds that booms in the prices of both stocks* and real estate are often accompanied by surges in the supply of credit and cross-border investment flows.[1] He also examines the relation between monetary authorities (the central bank in each country) and private-sector banks, and lenders. He concludes that the problem is not that large banks are unregulated, but that money can be too easy to borrow.[2] Such an expansive monetary environment is what causes banks to

> ❝ There is a biologic regularity in the pattern in each of these manias even though there are differences in details. ❞
>
> Charles P. Kindleberger, *Manias, Panics, and Crashes: A History of Financial Crises*

create more credit themselves and to purchase more loans—and eventually to go bust when the optimistic mania turns into a panic and crash.[3]

Kindleberger also dissects the stages of boom and bust.* This is the optimistic euphoria within a country's real estate or stock market that leads to speculators* borrowing more and more money to finance more investments, hoping for substantial short-term gains. As long as credit is easy to obtain, such professional speculators are always able to borrow more money to pay interest on outstanding loans. One ominous question echoes through Kindleberger's argument time and time again: "Where will borrowers get the money to pay the interest on their outstanding indebtedness if there are not enough new loans to provide the money?"[4] This leads him to his final theme: the importance of a "lender of last resort,"* which in today's global economy is needed at an international level to bail out large banks and firms to prevent or reduce the knock-on effects of their failure on the wider economy.

Exploring the Ideas

For Kindleberger, manias simply cannot be stopped. Once the financial world's "insiders" (investors with privileged access to the latest trends) start making money within a particular market, it's not long before "a follow-the-leader process develops as firms and households see that the investors make a lot of money." The reason behind this is emotive, not rational; there is "nothing as disturbing to one's well-being and judgment as to see a friend get rich. Unless it is a non-friend get richer."[5] These outsiders (Kindleberger's "non-friends") pour their money in, momentum develops, and soon a bubble* forms.[6] If credit is easily available, people will borrow wildly in order to make the most of the boom—and believe that this time, the good times will last (because "this time it's different.")[7] This recklessness pushes the bubble further, but because the behavior of every participant within it *seems* rational, no one can tell that the situation has become manic.[8] Cross-border investment flows (through international financial transactions like loans) add to the demand for "hot" investments, driving prices up even further. Nonetheless, authorities such as countries' central banks are often loathe to intervene, and take the "punch bowl away from the party just as the party is getting going," because they fear the public will react unfavorably to government interference.[9]

"The central question," Kindleberger writes, "is whether a central bank can restrain the instability in the supply of credit and slow speculation down to avoid its dangerous extension."[10] He doubts that central banks are "omniscient and omnipotent" (that is, all-knowing and all-powerful) enough to do this. That said, an international "lender of last resort" could help reduce the impact of such crises. When a banking crisis hits and banks are unexpectedly short of cash, they must sell their securities* to raise the necessary funds.[11] If all the banks are selling their securities at once, while all the other investors are likewise "running for the exits," then their capital* will not be significantly increased by these sales as prices will have already crashed. These banks might suddenly find themselves insolvent (that is, unable to meet their financial obligations, such as to honor debts).[12]

What a "lender of last resort" can do is extend cash loans to distressed institutions to see them through their cash crises, asking them to pay the loans back when the prices of their securities recover.

This spares the overall economy much of the turbulence and chaos of a more severe crash.

Language and Expression

Kindleberger saw himself as a "literary economist" who relied upon historical texts and narrative, much in the mold of the famous eighteenth-century philosopher and economist Adam Smith.*[13]

Although fairly technical wording does often appear in Kindleberger's writing, the technical material of *Manias, Panics, and Crashes* is mixed with a precise and enjoyable prose. It is also pitched at a readable tone of entertaining historical anecdote. For example, Kindleberger points out that some investors cannot resist investing in a known asset* bubble: prices are going up and they are convinced they will sell before the crash comes. To illustrate this point, he cites a banker who invested £500 (around £100,000 or $140,000 in today's terms) in the famous South Sea bubble* of 1720, saying, "When the rest of the world are mad, we must imitate them in some measure."[14] (During the South Sea bubble, shares in the British South Sea Company, granted a monopoly on trade with South America, rose to astronomical heights before crashing dramatically, damaging the British economy.) He follows this immediately with a quote from Chuck Prince,* then the chair of the US multinational finance corporation Citigroup, who said before the stock market crash of 2008* that "You have to keep dancing as long as the music is playing."[15]

This playfully suggests that such behavior in the world of finance has been consistent over time; and the pairing of these quotes gives them much greater impact than either would have had on its own. Together they speak directly to Kindleberger's primary point—that a "biologic regularity" exists within the manias, panics, and crashes of economic history.

NOTES

1   Charles P. Kindleberger and Robert Z. Aliber, *Manias, Panics, and Crashes: A History of Financial Crises* (Basingstoke: Palgrave MacMillan, 2015), 3.

2   Kindleberger and Aliber, *Manias, Panics, and Crashes*, 3.

3   Kindleberger and Aliber, *Manias, Panics, and Crashes*, 20.

4   Kindleberger and Aliber, *Manias, Panics, and Crashes*, 52.

5   Kindleberger and Aliber, *Manias, Panics, and Crashes*, 43.

6   Kindleberger and Aliber, *Manias, Panics, and Crashes*, 43.

7   Kindleberger and Aliber, *Manias, Panics, and Crashes*, 41.

8   Kindleberger and Aliber, *Manias, Panics, and Crashes*, 63.

9   Kindleberger and Aliber, *Manias, Panics, and Crashes*, 111.

10 Kindleberger and Aliber, *Manias, Panics, and Crashes*, 101.

11 Kindleberger and Aliber, *Manias, Panics, and Crashes*, 281.

12 Kindleberger and Aliber, *Manias, Panics, and Crashes*, 281.

13 Michael H. Turk, *The Idea of History in Constructing Economics* (Abingdon: Routledge, 2016), 191.

14 Kindleberger and Aliber, *Manias, Panics, and Crashes*, 57.

15 Kindleberger and Aliber, *Manias, Panics, and Crashes*, 57.

MODULE 6
SECONDARY IDEAS

KEY POINTS

- Kindleberger was concerned about how financial crises* often create currency crises* as well; he also saw that "positive feedback loops"*— self-amplifying cycles— within economies can make crises difficult to prevent.

- These secondary ideas build on Kindleberger's main points, illuminating the complex nature of financial crises.

- Currency crises underscore the international dimension to financial crises, while "positive feedback loops" reveal their durability.

Other Ideas

The secondary themes of Charles P. Kindleberger's *Manias, Panics, and Crashes: A History of Financial Crises* are the relationship between financial crises and currency crises, and what are known as "positive feedback loops." Besides the growth of cross-border investment flows,* Kindleberger saw other reasons for rising instability in the global economy. One was the United States's abandonment of the "gold standard"* in 1971.[1] The "gold standard" is a monetary system whereby a nation's currency has a value directly linked to a specific amount of gold. In 1934 the American government declared an ounce of gold to be worth $35, and held this ratio in place until 1971.

When a government's currency notes are backed by the inherent value of a precious metal like this, there are many stabilizing advantages. One is that the value of the currency will not rise or fall so turbulently in relation to other currencies (as it is anchored to gold, and so is "fixed.")* When the American dollar left the "gold standard" in 1971,

> **❝ By 1989 the chatter in Tokyo was that the market value of the land under the Imperial Palace was greater than the market value of all the real estate in California. ❞**
>
> Charles P. Kindleberger, *Manias, Panics, and Crashes: A History of Financial Crises*

it entered a "free-floating"* arrangement in which its value became much more strongly determined by international currency markets and their volatile forces of supply and demand.

Secondly, of all the "manias" from history examined by Kindleberger, the 1980s asset* bubble* in Japan* is among the most frequently mentioned. This example provides telling insights about the "positive feedback loops" of the boom-and-bust* cycle that make it so difficult to prevent: a boom creates more booms—in a way that seems failsafe and practically irresistible, thereby boosting investors'* and speculators'* confidence—while a bust creates self-feeding negativity that makes the crash worse and worse.[2]

Exploring the Ideas

Because of America's prominence in global capitalism* over the last decades, the dollar's gold standard was an anchor of stability for the entire global system ("capitalism" here refers to the social and economic system, increasingly dominant throughout the world, in which business and investment is conducted for private profit). Other countries could "peg" their currencies to the US dollar, continually revaluing their own respective currencies to maintain stable ratios of exchange with America (the dollar itself conferring a stable value in terms of gold). This provided much calmer currency exchange worldwide. The elaborate "Bretton Woods system,"* for example, in operation between 1945 and 1971, coordinated monetary management between the US, Canada, Western Europe, Australia, and Japan. It used the bedrock of the American gold standard to create stable exchange rates between these countries.

This dynamic was radically destabilized in 1971, however, when the US departure from the gold standard ended the Bretton Woods system. The dollar entered a "floating currency arrangement," whereby the international currency markets determined how valuable it was in relation to other currencies. International currency speculators can wreak havoc in such a market: if the mood of the crowd, seeking short-term profits, determines that the dollar is becoming less valuable in relation, say, to the British pound, a momentum can develop and soon the dollar can be devalued on the international marketplace for no reason other than that the irrational "herd" of speculators do not want to be left with a currency no one else wants.[3] Kindleberger predicted that America's change to a "floating" currency arrangement—disconnected from the stabilizing effects of the gold standard—would create a new source of financial instability.[4]

In the second half of the 1980s, the growth in the supplies of money and credit in Japan were extreme, and included an influx of global investment, which led to a boom in stock* and real estate prices.[5] Japanese banks owned large amounts of these two assets, so as the prices of stocks and real estate increased, the capital* of these banks also increased. The banks used this increase in capital to lend money to borrowers investing in stocks or real estate. Supplying money in the form of credit drove up the price of these assets even further, which in turn provided the lending banks with yet more capital (as the value of their own holdings increased again).[6] Through this process, "Japan had developed the financial equivalent of a 'perpetual motion machine.'" The more the banks lent out, the more they saw the price of their own assets rise, which gave them more money to lend out again.[7]

Naturally, when the crash finally hit, this "perpetual motion machine" began to work in reverse; stock and real estate prices fell, which meant the banks had less capital to loan money, which led to further reductions in price.[8] Japan's recession was severe and prolonged; it has not seen anything resembling such high growth and prosperity since.

Overlooked

While Kindleberger makes a compelling case for the dangers of free-floating currencies, it is possible to argue that this arrangement actually has benefits in terms of calming a "mania."

Economists like Milton Friedman* theorized that controlling a nation's money supply (the amount of money in circulation) is the best tool for controlling its economic performance. In boom times, a country can raise its interest rates.* This makes the cost of borrowing higher and therefore shrinks the money supply, restraining an overheated (and perhaps manic) economy. During recessionary times, a country might lower its interest rates, allowing money to be borrowed more cheaply and so providing a direct stimulus to the economy (when people spend the money they have borrowed).

But if a country is trying to maintain a fixed exchange rate with other countries (for example, by "pegging" their currency to the dollar), it is unable to increase or decrease the money supply in this way, as such a move will affect international supply and demand for that currency. If Argentina lowers its interest rates, say, and so increases its money supply, this will also increase the international supply of Argentinian pesos, making the currency less scarce. Everything else being equal, the value of the Argentinian peso will fall under these circumstances—a result acceptable under a free-floating system but not under a fixed one. In a fixed system, a particular pegged value of the Argentinian peso must be maintained by international agreement, which can prevent the government from lowering interest rates when it (perhaps desperately) needs to (if such a move will displace its currency from its agreed, pegged, international worth).

Therefore, a free-floating system can provide a country with the freedom to control its own money supply through interest rates—it is not obligated to maintain the value of its currency at any preordained, pegged level. Directly reducing the supply of money during excessively rapid growth can help weaken a boom, and so a free-floating exchange rate can actually encourage financial stability.

NOTES

1   Charles P. Kindleberger and Robert Z. Aliber, *Manias, Panics, and Crashes: A History of Financial Crises*, (Basingstoke: Palgrave MacMillan, 2015), 1.

2   Kindleberger and Aliber, *Manias, Panics, and Crashes*, 206.

3   Kindleberger and Aliber, *Manias, Panics, and Crashes*, 55–6.

4   Kindleberger and Aliber, *Manias, Panics, and Crashes*, 1.

5   Kindleberger and Aliber, *Manias, Panics, and Crashes*, 207.

6   Kindleberger and Aliber, *Manias, Panics, and Crashes*, 206.

7   Kindleberger and Aliber, *Manias, Panics, and Crashes*, 207.

8   Kindleberger and Aliber, *Manias, Panics, and Crashes*, 208.

MODULE 7
ACHIEVEMENT

KEY POINTS

- *Manias, Panics, and Crashes* is widely regarded as a pioneering study of financial crises,* and has become a classic in the field of economics.*

- Prophetically, *Manias, Panics, and Crashes* was published just before a series of intense financial crises, and offered observers a persuasive explanation as to what caused them.

- It could be argued that Kindleberger's thesis, which refutes the economic approach known as monetarism,* may not consider thoroughly enough how controlling the supply of money can be a stabilizing force in the world economy.

Assessing The Argument

The first edition of Charles P. Kindleberger's *Manias, Panics, and Crashes: A History of Financial Crises* was published in 1978. It is fair to say that—even though the book leans on the work of his predecessor, the economist Hyman Minsky*—Kindleberger achieved his ambitions and created his own classic book on financial catastrophes on an international scale. His immense weight of learning is evident throughout, not only through well-chosen examples of financial crises and contemporary quotes, but also in the way he presents them within a description of the stages of boom and bust.*

As global economies grow increasingly interdependent, there remains much to be learned from Kindleberger's ideas of "international propagation" (or contagion),* according to which "financial crises often ricochet from one country to another."[1] This groundbreaking perspective has been increasingly validated and cited since 1978; a

> **❝** More manias, panics, and crashes may plague us, but readers of this book will at least have been inoculated. **❞**
>
> Robert M. Solow, foreword to *Manias, Panics, and Crashes: A History of Financial Crises*

recent and wide-ranging assessment of Kindleberger's achievement, funded by the European Union, was another notable moment in this process of critical affirmation.[2] Kindleberger also succeeded in expressing his ideas with engaging writing, earning him the moniker "literary economist." The economics editor of Princeton University Press referred to his book as a "model for economists who want to reach a wider audience," thanks to his refined yet accessible style.[3]

Since 1978, *Manias, Panics, and Crashes* has gone through seven editions to date, each building on the last—the most recent editions have been edited and updated by Robert Z. Aliber—and Kindleberger has been repeatedly praised as a giant in his field. The text is still frequently quoted by investors, academics, politicians, and journalists. The British newspaper the *Financial Times*, for example, referred to Kindleberger as "the pre-eminent historian of financial crises" almost 10 years after his death in 2003.[4] The popular financial book *Code Red: How to Protect Your Savings From the Coming Crisis* (2013) by economists John Maudlin* and Jonathan Tepper* calls Kindleberger's classic text "the bible on bubbles."*[5]

Achievement in Context

Undoubtedly, part of the great success of *Manias, Panics, and Crashes* is down to timing. When the first edition was published in 1978, some of the biggest bubbles and crashes in economic history were about to take place. Throughout the 1970s there had been a surge in loans (that is, credit) from international banks to governments and government-owned firms in Mexico, Brazil, Argentina, and 10 other developing countries[6] ("developing"here refers to their state of national prosperity, considered less advanced than in "developed" nations such as the United States or Germany). The external indebtedness of these countries was increasing by 20 percent a year, and consequently, in 1982, they defaulted on their combined debts of $800 billion.[7] This sparked financial crises within each of these nations, as well as in the international banks that had funded them. As the Lebanese American author and investor Nassim Nicholas Taleb* puts it so memorably in his book *Black Swan* (2007): "In the summer of 1982, large American banks lost close to all their past earnings (cumulatively), about everything they ever made in the history of American banking— everything," due to this unexpected wave of defaults.*[8]

Global crises followed in other parts of the world, including the bubble in stocks and real estate in Japan (1985–9);* the East Asian crisis* (1997); the dot.com boom* in the American stock market concerning technology companies (1995–9); and the bubble in real estate in the US, UK, Spain, Ireland, and Iceland (2002–7). Each crisis was triggered by a huge surge in credit, and, as the 2015 edition of *Manias, Panics, and Crashes* points out, these "surges in the credit supply appear to be becoming larger."[9]

Throughout these troublesome decades, the work of both Kindleberger and Hyman Minsky have received more attention. The relevance of Kindleberger's book continues to grow in the eyes of the financial community, and each succeeding edition has benefitted from more urgent, contemporary material to analyze and digest.[10]

Limitations

If *Manias, Panics, and Crashes* has one major limitation, it is its lack of ideas as to how future financial crises can be prevented. Kindleberger can be persuasive in dismissing popular remedies for reckless lending behavior; for example, he denies that increased regulation is the answer. Like other aspects of his argument, this stance is rooted in historical evidence; he reminds the reader that, "Although banks have been regulated for more than three hundred years, the universal response to failure or near failure of banks is that more regulation or more effective regulation is needed."[11] His position also rests on the idea that, because manias result from the excessively rapid growth of credit, there is no regulation that is suited to solving the problem;[12] such manic periods are intimately associated with the practice of capitalism*—which relies on the creation of credit in order to function. Any attempt to regulate the economy by limiting credit could sink the entire system into a permanent recession.

There is an obvious defeatism in this statement. Not all regulation is equal, and while a new era may present new problems, it may also offer new solutions. The Nobel Prize*–winning economist Paul Krugman* has refuted Kindleberger's attitude towards regulation, arguing that new US banking regulations after the Great Depression* gave the country "a workable solution, involving both guarantees and oversight" and provided a half-century of financial stability.[13] Krugman passionately argues that such governance can be updated to today's needs, whereas Kindleberger's book stoically accepts reckless behavior. Kindleberger might be passionate about the need for a "lender of last resort"* to rescue a country from financial crisis (preventing a bad situation from becoming a full-on global disaster), but he seems resigned to the belief that serious economic crises are an inevitable aspect of the capitalist system.

NOTES

1   Charles P. Kindleberger and Robert Z. Aliber, *Manias, Panics, and Crashes: A History of Financial Crises* (Basingstoke: Palgrave MacMillan, 2015),185.

2   Piero Pasotti and Alessandro Vercelli, "Kindleberger and Financial Crises," *Financialisation, Economy, Society, and Sustainable Development Working Paper Series* 104 (February, 2015), accessed March 22, 2016, http:// fessud.eu/wp-content/uploads/2015/01/Kindleberger-and-Financial-Crises-Fessud-final_Working-Paper-104.pdf.

3   *Economist*, "Of Manias, Panics, and Crashes," July 19, 2003, accessed March 22, 2016, http:/www.economist.com/node/1923462.

4   Ashoka Mody, "Germany must lead by example on fixing its banks," *Financial Times*, May 27, 2013, accessed March 22, 2016, http:// www.ft.com/intl/cms/s/0/10e7ccbe-c46f-11e2-9ac0-00144feab7de. html#axzz43Y4Huy4b.

5   John Maudlin and Jonathan Tepper, *Code Red: How to Protect Your Savings From the Coming Crisis* (Hoboken: John Wiley & Sons, 2013), 193.

6   Kindleberger and Aliber, *Manias, Panics, and Crashes*, 1.

7   Kindleberger and Aliber, *Manias, Panics, and Crashes*, 5.

8   Nassim Nicholas Taleb, *The Black Swan: The Impact of the Highly Improbable* (London: Penguin, 2007), 43.

9   Kindleberger and Aliber, *Manias, Panics, and Crashes*, 16.

10 Two examples of Kindleberger's continued prominence: *Economist*, "Of Manias, Panics, and Crashes;" and Paul Krugman, "China Bites the Cherry," *New York Times*, August 12, 2015, accessed March 22, 2016, http:// krugman.blogs.nytimes.com/2015/08/12/china-bites-the-cherry/?_r=0.

11 Kindleberger and Aliber, *Manias, Panics, and Crashes*, 239.

12 Kindleberger and Aliber, *Manias, Panics, and Crashes*, 239.

13 Paul Krugman, "Why We Regulate," *New York Times*, May 13, 2012, accessed March 22, 2016, http:/www.nytimes.com/2012/05/14/opinion/ krugman-why-we-regulate.html.

MODULE 8
PLACE IN THE AUTHOR'S WORK

KEY POINTS

- Kindleberger's work demonstrates a long-standing engagement with financial crises* through a distinctly international perspective.

- His 1973 book *The World in Depression*, 1929–1939 was published five years before *Manias, Panics and Crashes*, and laid the foundations for the arguments he develops in the later book.

- While Kindleberger was already a highly esteemed economist, Manias, Panics, and Crashes solidified his reputation and legacy.

Positioning

Charles P. Kindleberger's *Manias, Panics, and Crashes: A History of Financial Crises* may build directly on the ideas of the US economist Hyman Minsky,* but it also advances his own earlier work.

In 1973, Kindleberger published *The World in Depression, 1929–1939*, which argued that the Great Depression* in the 1930s was wide, deep, and prolonged because there had been no international "lender of last resort"* to bail out failing financial institutions such as struggling banks.[1] The book was radical in that it departed from the US-centric perspective that had dominated the subject. As fellow economists have noted, "While much of the earlier literature, often authored by Americans, focused on the Great Depression in the US, Kindleberger emphasized that the Depression had a prominent international and, in particular, European dimension."[2]

A "lender of last resort," Kindleberger argued, could have calmed the panic and crash that led to the Great Depression, but the world was

> ❝ Kindleberger's argument grew out of his interpretation of the Great Depression. ❞
>
> Lord Robert Skidelsky, afterword to *Manias, Panics, and Crashes: A History of Financial Crises*

at an awkward crossroads. Britain, the previous leader of the world economy, was too weak to fulfill this role after World War I* (1914–18) and America, the rising new leader of the world, was unwilling to assume such responsibility.[3] Consequently, the "negative feedback loop"*—vicious circle—of the global crash was allowed to get worse and worse, with no "lender of last resort" to put the brakes on an economic train wreck.

Kindleberger saw a strong parallel between this lack of American leadership in the 1930s and its lack of leadership in the 1970s, when the global system was faltering due to the collapse of the "gold standard"* and the Bretton Woods system.* These two mechanisms had, in Kindleberger's eyes, provided much-needed stability to the global economy—but in 1971 the United States abandoned the gold standard, which in turn led to the abandonment of the Bretton Woods system of foreign exchange. For Kindleberger, this sowed the seeds of future instability.[4] Given subsequent financial crises, it can easily be argued that he was right.

Integration

Kindleberger's distinguished career began with an interest in foreign exchange. His first book, *International Short-Term Capital Movements* (1937), examined how capital*—financial resources—was being moved around the world by speculators* to earn higher interest rates. It also explored the international debts that were accumulated by changes in the international balance of payments* (whether a country was a "creditor" or "debtor" to the rest of the world).[5] *The Dollar*

Shortage (1950) addressed the relationship between a country's level of economic development and its international balance of payments.[6]

This earlier focus on international trade perhaps explains the uniquely international perspective that Kindleberger brought to *The World in Depression, 1929–1939* and *Manias, Panics, and Crashes*. In this sense, his preoccupations with international capital movements and balance of payments remained consistent throughout his career, steadily expanding to a much wider view of economic and financial history. By the 1970s Kindleberger was focusing on the nature of financial crises, past and present, with a particular eye on panics, contagion,* and the need for an international "lender of last resort."

Significance

Manias, Panics, and Crashes was highly significant to Kindleberger's career and legacy. An esteemed economics* professor at the Massachusetts Institute of Technology (MIT),* his reputation was already secure thanks to his previous work and publications, most notably *The World in Depression, 1929–1939*. Praised by the famous Canadian-born economist John Kenneth Galbraith,* this book is a classic in its own right.[7]

With *Manias, Panics, and Crashes*, Kindleberger became regarded as a pioneer in his field. In 1978, he proclaimed the increased fragility of the new global economy due to the collapse of the US gold standard and international Bretton Woods system. It was just at this moment, in the late 1970s and early 1980s, that the full impact of this fragility would be felt within the global economy, and be sustained for the next 30-plus years. Between 1982 and 2007, the global economy would experience six of the ten biggest financial bubbles* in the history of markets.[8] Kindleberger's book "paved the way" in analyzing the sources of these crises, and in considering what can be done to minimize their impact on the global economic system.[9] His book came to rival, and probably surpass *The World in Depression* in both its achievement and popularity—although it is undoubtedly an extension of the ideas explored in that earlier study.

NOTES

1   Charles P. Kindleberger and Robert Z. Aliber, *Manias, Panics, and Crashes: A History of Financial Crises* (Basingstoke: Palgrave MacMillan, 2015), 24.

2   Piero Pasotti and Alessandro Vercelli, "Kindleberger and Financial Crises," *Financialisation, Economy, Society, and Sustainable Development Working Paper Series* 104 (February, 2015), accessed March 22, 2016, http://fessud.eu/wp-content/uploads/2015/01/Kindleberger-and-Financial-Crises-Fessud-final_Working-Paper-104.pdf: 6.

3   Charles P. Kindleberger, *The World in Depression, 1929–1939* (Berkeley; Los Angeles: University of California Press, 1973), 292.

4   Kindleberger, *The World in Depression*, 308.

5   Charles P. Kindleberger, *International Short-Term Capital Movements* (New York: Columbia University Press, 1937).

6   Charles P. Kindleberger, *The Dollar Shortage* (New York: John Wiley & Sons, 1950).

7   Kindleberger, *The World in Depression, 1929–1939*, 1.

8   Kindleberger and Aliber, *Manias, Panics, and Crashes*, 18.

9   Sakis Gekas, "Different Because Worse," *Dublin Review of Books* 16 (Winter 2010), accessed March 22, 2016, http://www.drb.ie/essays/different-because-worse.

SECTION 3
IMPACT

MODULE 9
THE FIRST RESPONSES

KEY POINTS

- While Kindleberger appeals for an international "lender of last resort"* to bail out large financial institutions that are struggling, he does not specify what this entity should look like in reality.

- Subsequent financial crises* showed that such a "lender of last resort" was indeed needed, and these events were incorporated into new editions of *Manias, Panics, and Crashes*.

- Given that the world economy grew more volatile after the publication of *Manias, Panics, and Crashes*, more people became convinced of irrational investment behavior—and by Kindleberger's argument.

Criticism

Upon publication in 1978, *Manias, Panics, and Crashes: A History of Financial Crises* was generally praised by peer reviews, although flaws were also mentioned. One 1979 issue of the *Economic History Review* applauded the "immense weight of learning" that Charles P. Kindleberger had brought to such an "apparently wild" subject, and said that it yielded new insights.[1] But the review also questioned the book's conclusion, criticizing Kindleberger's emphasis on the need for an international "lender of last resort," without explaining what form it should take.[2]

The *Economic Journal* also lauded the balance that Kindleberger achieved between scholarliness and style, but was unconvinced by his basic assumption that the "euphoric" periods of a mania reflected "irrational" behavior on the part of investors* and institutions.[3] This

> ❝ Kindleberger's enthusiasm for lenders of last resort is vague. ❞
>
> Patrick Minford, *"Manias, Panics, and Crashes. A History of Financial Crises.* By Charles P. Kindleberger," *Economic Journal*

early review maintained that this behavior is compatible with market efficiency,* and so sided with the efficient market hypothesis* that was in vogue at the time (and at odds with Kindleberger's ideas).[4] The reviewer also found Kindleberger's enthusiasm for a "lender of last resort" to be "vague," and disparaged his "literary economics," referring to the work's accessible narrative writing style.[5]

Responses

When Kindleberger wrote *Manias, Panics, and Crashes*, the academic environment was largely loyal to the efficient market hypothesis and its assumption that investors' behavior tends to be rational. Given his observation that it is in fact far from rational, Kindleberger issued a major challenge to orthodox thinking in his field. He persisted with his argument through several subsequent, revised editions of his book, and eventually the critics caught up with its conclusions.

Reviewers of the first edition of *Manias, Panics, and Crashes* noticed that most of Kindleberger's (many) examples of past financial crises came from the period 1719–1929, "with some reference to more recent events."[6] However, with the financial crisis of 1982,* a new era of economic turbulence and fragility began. Kindleberger and, after his death in 2003, his successor Robert Z. Aliber* responded with six new editions of *Manias, Panics, and Crashes* from 1989 to 2015. Each of these editions had a wealth of new material to draw on, analyze, and compare. For example, the 1996 edition included analyses of the US stock market crash of 1987* ("Black Monday," when nervousness in the markets following a short conflict between the United States and

Iran saw a plunge in the value of shares) and the 1995 peso devaluation*
(following the Mexican government's decision to devalue the peso
against the US dollar by 15 percent, investors sought to sell their
investments in Mexico; the consequence was a crisis that spread to the
Asian markets). The 2000 edition included an examination of the
1997 East Asian crisis,* which began in Thailand and then spread
quickly to other East Asian countries. None of the new case studies
stand alone; they each become part of the larger argument about
financial crises, the "biologic regularity"* (a set of consistent stages of
development) they all share, and what can be done about them.

It was not long before Kindleberger's appeal for an international
"lender of last resort" also found more support. The political scientist
Robert Keohane* developed the thesis and rebranded it "the theory
of hegemonic* stability"—a label that stuck over time[7] ("hegemonic"
here refers to the dominance of a political or economic superpower).
Keohane himself noticed a growing literature centered on this topic
and surveyed it in his book *After Hegemony: Cooperation and Discord in
the World of Political Economy* (1984).[8] A new conversation had begun.

Conflict and Consensus

As time passed, *Manias, Panics, and Crashes* became regarded as a
"classic" by most of the academic and financial community.[9] Even
while admiring Kindleberger's study, however, such critics still take
issue with central aspects of it, such as its failure to define "financial
crises."[10] While Kindleberger himself admitted that this key term
might be beyond any sort of precise and generally agreed clarification,
critics have insisted on its absolute necessity.[11] Likewise, the book says
little about the distinction between crises that have led to depressions
and those that have not.[12]

Beyond such disputes over the actual content of the book, large
theoretical challenges also remain. The efficient market hypothesis has
not gone away, and its greatest publicist—the economist and author

Burton G. Malkiel*— extols its virtues in his recent best selling book *A Random Walk Down Wall Street* (the latest edition of which was also published in 2015). In Malkiel's eyes, in a "mania" investors will realize sooner or later the true value of their assets,* and act accordingly— that is to say, rationally: "While the stock market in the short run may be a voting mechanism, in the long run it is a weighing mechanism. True value will win out in the end."[13] Kindleberger and his successor and updater, Aliber, do not have much time for any form of the efficient market hypothesis; according to Aliber's 2015 edition, the EMH implies "clairvoyance" on the part of investors.[14]

NOTES

1 W. Ashworth, "*Manias, Panics, and Crashes: A History of Financial Crises* by Charles P. Kindleberger," *Economic History Review* 32, no. 3 (1979): 421–2.

2 Ashworth, "*Manias, Panics, and Crashes,*" 422.

3 Patrick Minford, "*Manias, Panics, and Crashes. A History of Financial Crises* by Charles P. Kindleberger," *Economic Journal* 89 (December, 1979): 947.

4 Minford, "*Manias, Panics, and Crashes,*" 947.

5 Minford, "*Manias, Panics, and Crashes,*" 947, 948.

6 Ashworth, "*Manias, Panics, and Crashes,*" 421.

7 Stephen Meardon, "On Kindleberger and Hegemony: From Berlin to M.I.T. and Back," *Bowdoin Digital Commons*, September 29, 2013, accessed March 22, 2016, http://digitalcommons.bowdoin.edu/cgi/viewcontent.cgi?article=1003&context=econpapers.

8 Meardon, "On Kindleberger and Hegemony."

9 See Christopher Kobrak and Mira Wilkins, *History and Financial Crisis: Lessons from the 20th Century* (New York: Routledge, 2013), 3. For an example from the financial community, see Jason Zweig, "Read It and Reap: The Best Books for Investors," *Wall Street Journal*, November 28, 2014, accessed March 22, 2016, http://www.wsj.com/articles/read-it-and-reap-the-best-books-for-investors-1417213387.

10 Kobrak and Wilkins, *History and Financial Crises*, 3.

11 Kobrak and Wilkins, *History and Financial Crises,* 4.

12 Richard Sylla, "Financial Disturbances and Depressions: The View from Economic History," Social Science Research Network: Levy Economics Institute Working Paper 47 (April 1991): 3.

13 Burton G. Malkiel, "The Efficient Market Hypothesis and Its Critics," *Journal of Economic Perspectives* 17, no. 1 (2003): 61.

14 Charles P. Kindleberger and Robert Z. Aliber, *Manias, Panics, and Crashes: A History of Financial Crises* (Basingstoke: Palgrave MacMillan, 2015), 53–6.

MODULE 10
THE EVOLVING DEBATE

KEY POINTS

- As financial crises* mounted over time, Kindleberger's ideas, particularly his call for an international "lender of last resort"* capable of bailing out large financial institutions that find themselves in trouble were taken more seriously.

- A general theory of "hegemonic* stability"—a stability founded on the dominance of a single nation—evolved to address what such a "lender of last resort" would look like.

- Since the publication of *Manias, Panics, Crashes*, the discipline of economics* has embraced the study of irrational investment behavior through new fields like behavioral economics,* which draws on the field of psychology*—the study of the mind and behavior—to explain economic decision-making.

Uses And Problems

Charles P. Kindleberger's view of financial crises in *Manias, Panics, and Crashes: A History of Financial Crises* ultimately calls for serious policy coordination at a global level. That said, and as critics of Kindleberger have noted, his vision of what an international "lender of last resort" should look like in real life can sometimes seem vague.

From the 1980s onward economists and political scientists, inspired by Kindleberger's ideas, began to meet the challenge of designing such an entity. The US political scientist Robert Keohane* began to envision a real-life, international "lender of last resort" in his book *After Hegemony: Cooperation and Discord in the World of Political Economy* (1984).[1] The distinguished economist Barry Eichengreen* wrote "Hegemonic Stability Theories of the International Monetary

> **“**Innovations that have transformed finance over the past decade have substantially improved the overall stability and resilience of the US financial system. But these improvements are unlikely to have brought an end to what Charles Kindleberger called 'manias and panics.' **”**
>
> Timothy F. Geithner, "Change and Challenges Facing the US Financial System," *BIS Review*

System" in 1987, in which he examined the conditions, institutions, and degree of leadership necessary to achieve international monetary coordination.[2] This issue would become an abiding interest for Eichengreen, while Robert Gilpin,* a scholar of economic relations on the international scale, published *The Political Economy of International Relations* (1987), influenced by Kindleberger's position. This book examined America's leadership in the global financial structure after World War II* and how it had since declined. For Gilpin, the US is absolutely central to the creation of international financial cooperation.[3] These, and many other such studies inspired by Kindleberger, demonstrate how his insights have been used. Thinkers influenced by Kindleberger recognize that financial crises are international in nature, and tend to conclude that stabilizing them calls for new international cooperation. Achieving this is an ongoing challenge—perhaps made even more difficult in the current age of growing economic nationalism*—an ideology in which a nation considers its own economic health to be entirely, and uncompromisingly, paramount at the expense of the global economy's overall health.

Schools of Thought

Manias, Crashes, and Panics was first published during the heyday of the efficient market hypothesis,* with its assumption that investors* behave rationally. The book directly diverged from the dominant way of thinking about the nature of the economic cycles that lead to catastrophes. When the world experienced a series of financial crises, starting with that of 1982,* Kindleberger's work suddenly seemed spot on: a new recognition of bubbles* and irrational investment behavior turned the established way of thinking on its head.[4] Behavioral economics, for example, is a rapidly evolving field that emerged through this period: it holds that investors are generally far from rational, and instead reflect psychological biases such as overconfidence, prejudiced judgments, and herd mentality. Like Kindleberger, behavioral economists believe (and worry) that such behavior makes bubbles self-fulfilling, in the sense that when everyone thinks asset* prices will rise, they buy assets, thereby causing the prices to rise; when everyone thinks prices are going to fall, they sell, and prices tumble.[5]

Academics exploring how an international "lender of last resort" could work politically form a broader school of thought. They are engaged in an ongoing debate that includes many politicians as well, often working on strategies to solve real-life crises. In his memoir, for example, former US treasury secretary Timothy Geithner* recalls warning investment banks against complacency in 2004, quoting from *Manias, Panics, and Crashes*, and says that the book deeply influenced his own views on financial crises.[6]

In Current Scholarship

Since Kindleberger's death in 2003, the economist Robert Z. Aliber* has edited and updated subsequent editions of *Manias, Panics, and Crashes*. In this role he now shares ownership and development of the book's project, adding new examples of financial crises and irrational behavior to its already vast panorama.

In the seventh, and to date the most recent, edition, Aliber takes the book's argument one step further in an inventive turn of his own. He examines a sequence of financial crises that have taken place one after the other over the past 40 years—first the Mexico and South American financial crisis of the early 1980s,* then the Japanese crash of 1990,* then the East Asian crisis* of 1997, and finally the real estate crashes affecting several countries in 2007 and 2008.* He argues that these successive "waves" of credit-fueled booms and busts* were causally related.[7] When the international money feeding one mania suddenly fled the country and panic set in, most of this money was moved to another international location to begin pumping up another (ill-fated) boom.[8] Aliber's point is that roughly the same international money, sloshing around the world and guided by institutions such as large global banks, was behind each of these booms and the consequent busts. This is a bold, highly specific argument in the spirit of Kindleberger's original thesis.

Beyond Aliber's scholarly development of Kindleberger's argument, discussion of it is widespread throughout the worlds of academia, finance, politics, and journalism. The work enjoys high esteem in the business world as well; one private business advisory group even profiles the book on its website, proclaiming that it should be "a regular staple for all, from central bankers to ordinary bankers, from investors to regular businessmen and women, in the halls of government and in the average living room."[9] Kindleberger's ideas are now widely accepted in multiple spheres, and are praised for their precision, foresight, and continuing relevance worldwide.

NOTES

1   Robert Keohane, *After Hegemony: Cooperation and Discord in the World of Political Economy* (Princeton: Princeton University Press, 1984).

2   Eichengreen, Barry, "Hegemonic Stability Theories of the International Monetary System," in *Can Nations Agree? Issues in International Economic Cooperation* by Richard Cooper et al, (Washington, DC: Brookings Institution, 1989): 255–98.

3   Robert Gilpin, *The Political Economy of International Relations* (Princeton: Princeton University Press, 1987).

4   *Economist*, "Of Manias, Panics, and Crashes," July 19, 2003, accessed March 22, 2016, http://www.economist.com/node/1923462.

5   Todd A. Knoop, *Business Cycle Economics: Understanding Recessions and Depressions from Boom to Bust* (Santa Barbara, CA: Praeger, 2015), 172.

6   Timothy F. Geithner, *Stress Test: Reflections on Financial Crises* (New York: Crown Publishers, 2014).

7   Charles P. Kindleberger and Robert Z. Aliber, *Manias, Panics, and Crashes: A History of Financial Crises* (Basingstoke: Palgrave MacMillan, 2015), ix.

8   Kindleberger and Aliber, *Manias, Panics, and Crashes*, ix.

9   Gail Fosler, "Lessons from Kindleberger on the Financial Crisis," The Gail Fosler Group, April 28, 2013, accessed March 22, 2016, http://www.gailfosler.com/lessons-from-kindleberger-on-the-financial-crisis.

MODULE 11
IMPACT AND INFLUENCE TODAY

KEY POINTS

- *Manias, Panics, and Crashes* remains a popular classic in economics.

- The question as to how to contain financial crises* is still a challenge to today's economists and policymakers.

- Whether fixed exchange rates* are part of the solution is still a subject of debate.

Position

Charles P. Kindleberger's *Manias, Panics, and Crashes: A History of Financial Crises* remains influential and relevant almost 40 years after it was first published in 1978. It is still frequently mentioned in relation to current events—for example, when the Chinese stock market crashed in the summer of 2015, the British economic journal the *Economist* opened a feature on this news with a direct link to Kindleberger's framework: "The great Charles Kindleberger described the pattern of how bubbles form and then burst in his book *Manias, Panics and Crashes*."[1]

Kindleberger's appeals have clearly been heard at the highest possible levels of political economy. In the foreword to *Manias, Panics and Crashes*, the US economist Robert M. Solow* remarks that Kindleberger "would certainly have been fascinated—and probably gratified—by the way the Federal Reserve* acted during the [2008] crisis not only as lender of last resort* to the banking system but almost as lender of last resort to the whole economy."[2] Furthermore, in the 40th anniversary edition of Kindleberger's earlier book, *The World in Depression, 1929–1939,* its editors note the continuing importance of

> ❝ The most rigorous—and certainly the greatest—book of its kind, Charles Kindleberger's definitive *Manias, Panics and Crashes.* ❞
>
> Nick Murray, "A Treasure Trove Of Financial Folly," *Financial Advisor*

his "theory of hegemonic* stability" during a period of global financial crisis and US political dysfunction.[3] The publisher's description of the book highlights its use by major players in global economic politics: "This masterpiece of economic history shows why US treasury secretary Lawrence Summers,* during the darkest hours of the 2008 Global Financial Crisis,* turned to Kindleberger and his peers for guidance."[4]

Interaction

Countries can still choose whether to have fixed or free-floating currencies.* While Kindleberger sees fixed exchange rates as more stable, this has been seriously challenged by the International Monetary Fund's* research, which discovered no empirical differences in volatility between the two systems.[5] The International Monetary Fund (IMF) is an institution founded to secure international financial stability and cooperation; it commonly lends money to nations in financial distress in return for structural changes to their economies such as the implementation of spending cuts or the privatization of state-owned businesses.

The debate over who is to blame for the financial crisis of 2008* also continues, with Lehman Brothers* (the New York-based investment bank that went bankrupt in 2008) often cast as the scapegoat. Kindleberger would see Lehman Brothers as a small player in a much larger dynamic: one in which the supply of credit was surging across the board, and investors* were entering a "euphoric" phase of irrationally optimistic forecasts.[6]

More generally, the basic premise of *Manias, Panics, and Crashes*—that there is a "biologic regularity"* to financial crises that has been consistent throughout history, with oversupply of credit being the primary issue—has been refuted by a vast number of critics still analyzing the 2008 crash. Many of them see the crash as having been a totally unique product of its time, with little in common with other financial crises from history.

The Continuing Debate

In his later career, Kindleberger consistently saw the end of the US gold standard* and the mechanisms of financial relations between nations that defined the Bretton Woods system* in the early 1970s, and conversion of the dollar and many other currencies to a free-floating arrangement, as a new source of global economic instability. A 2004 paper from the International Monetary Fund directly challenged this view. It found that in the 30 preceding years, the volatility of fixed exchange rates was about the same as that of floating rates—something that is possible because a currency pegged to the US dollar must still go up and down with the US dollar against the world's other (non-pegged) currencies.[7] More than this, the study showed that a volatile currency had very little effect on international trade flows going in and out of a country.[8] This means that a fixed exchange rate system may not provide the kind of stability Kindleberger envisioned.

Many prominent thinkers and writers continue to ignore Kindleberger's insights when analyzing the crash of 2008. Lehman Brothers is still often cast as the source of the crisis: popular books have been published with titles such as *A Colossal Failure of Common Sense: The Inside Story of the Collapse of Lehman Brothers* (2009) by the bank's former vice-chairman Lawrence G. McDonald* and the economist Patrick Robinson;* and the journalist Vicky Ward's* *The Devil's Casino: Friendship, Betrayal, and the High Stakes Games Played Inside Lehman Brothers* (2010).[9]

Other causes have been pinpointed as the "true" source of the crisis by thinkers who see these factors as completely unique to 2008. Financial journalist Scott Patterson's* book *The Quants* (2010) argues that Wall Street's math-minded "quantitative analysts" took over much of the financial system in the year preceding the crash, and were responsible for it.[10] One trader from this era was bold enough to publish the book *How I Caused the Credit Crunch* (2009), implying that he was solely responsible.[11] None of these books view the crash from Kindleberger's much wider, historic perspective.

NOTES

1 Buttonwood, "China's Stockmarket: The Great Leap Backward," *Economist*, July 8, 2015, accessed March 22, 2016, http://www.economist.com/blogs/buttonwood/2015/07/chinas-stockmarket.

2 Charles P. Kindleberger and Robert Z. Aliber, *Manias, Panics, and Crashes: A History of Financial Crises* (Basingstoke: Palgrave MacMillan, 2015), viii.

3 Charles P. Kindleberger, *The World in Depression, 1929–1939*, ed. J. Bradford DeLong and Barry Eichengreen (Berkeley; Los Angeles: University of California Press, 2013), ix.

4 University of California Press, "*The World in Depression, 1929–1939*," accessed March 22, 2016, http://www.ucpress.edu/book.php?isbn=9780520275850.

5 Peter Clark, et al., "Exchange Rate Volatility and Trade Flows - Some New Evidence," International Monetary Fund (May 2004): 54–5, accessed March 21, 2016, https://www.imf.org/external/np/res/exrate/2004/eng/051904.pdf.

6 Kindleberger and Aliber, *Manias, Panic, and Crashes,* 15.

7 Clark et al., "Exchange Rate Volatility," 54–5.

8   Clark et al., "Exchange Rate Volatility," 55.

9   Lawrence G. McDonald with Patrick Robinson, *A Colossal Failure of Common Sense: The Inside Story of the Collapse of Lehman Brothers* (New York: Three Rivers Press, 2009); Vicky Ward, *The Devil's Casino: Friendship, Betrayal, and the High-Stakes Games Played Inside Lehman Brothers* (Hoboken: John Wiley & Sons, 2010).

10 Scott Patterson, *The Quants: How a New Breed of Math Whizzes Conquered Wall Street and Nearly Destroyed It* (New York: Crown Business, 2010).

11 Tetsuya Ishikawa, *How I Caused the Credit Crunch: An Insider's Story of the Financial Meltdown* (London: Icon Books, 2009).

MODULE 12
WHERE NEXT?

KEY POINTS

- Kindleberger's text looks set to remain a touchstone for economists and politicians seeking to stabilize the world economy.

- *Manias, Panics, and Crashes* is an evolving text that illustrates exactly how financial crises* work, and that provides an arena for possible solutions to global economic upheaval.

- *Manias, Panics, and Crashes* explains the cycle of boom and bust* in a way that is historically grounded, of the moment, and enduringly human.

Potential

In today's contexts, the importance and influence of Charles P. Kindleberger's work looks set to endure, especially since these contexts so closely (and frighteningly) mirror the concerns that *Manias, Panics, and Crashes: A History of Financial Crises* foreshadowed in the 1970s. For example, the Chinese stock market crashed on June 12, 2015 with the value of the Shanghai stock exchange sinking by a third.[1] After a period of stabilization, the same market crashed again at the start of 2016 and triggered a global retreat of stock markets.[2] Meanwhile, the bubble* in oil prices also burst, incurring huge deflationary* pressures on the world economy—a rise in the value of money, experienced as a fall in prices.

All of this was big news, and Kindleberger's text was one of the most frequently mentioned by its commentators. Regarding China's 2015 stock market crash, two distinguished professors from the

> **❝** China's problem is much like that of Japan's in the early 1990s; the amount that households wish to save is much larger than business firms can profitably invest. **❞**
>
> Robert Z. Aliber, *Manias, Panics, and Crashes: A History of Financial Crises*

University of Hong Kong stated that "Though the blame game is ongoing, the historian Charles Kindleberger's 1978 book *Manias, Panics, and Crashes: A History of Financial Crises* offers the perfect explanation of what China is experiencing."[3] Speaking about the collapse in oil prices, one commentator writes that "the energy cycle fits the classic scenario that Professor Kindleberger described in his classic history of financial manias, *Manias, Panics, and Crashes*."[4] These examples reflect just a snippet of Kindleberger's enduring presence in contemporary conversations about the most significant global economic events. If anything, the book continues to gain relevance over time.

Future Directions

New editions of *Manias, Panics, and Crashes* have continued to be issued since Kindleberger's death in 2003, including much new material and analysis; his argument continues to evolve. The book's current coauthor and editor, University of Chicago professor Robert Z. Aliber,* added an epilogue to the 2015 edition that focuses on China, warning that its high rates of growth are actually a bubble ready to burst, especially as so much of the country's growth has been built on credit. The events of early 2016, with the Chinese stock market falling steeply and prompting a global sell-off of shares, could be viewed as this shift from the "manic" stage of Kindleberger's cycle to the "panic." One American academic has said that, given these events in China, "[t]he need for an eighth edition of *Manias, Panics and Crashes* may soon be apparent."[5] Aliber has picked up the baton from Kindleberger; the discussion that *Manias, Panics, and Crashes* began in 1978 rages on in ever wider circles and—given the state of the global economy—with increasing urgency.

Kindleberger's central recommendation to soothe volatile (unstable) markets is the establishment of an international "lender of last resort."* Although a global financial institution existed when Kindleberger first formulated his position, he was not convinced that it could sufficiently fill the "institutional vacuum" he identified. The International Monetary Fund* (IMF) was established in the 1940s to act as such an international "lender of last resort."[6] However, many economists question how effective it is, asking "whether the presence of the IMF as a supplier of national currencies to countries with financial crises encouraged profligate national financial policies."[7]

Ultimately, the IMF or any international "lender of last resort" must pull off a difficult balancing act: it must be there and ready to lend in the case of financial crises, but it must always make the delivery of such help uncertain, so that its presence does not encourage reckless behavior.[8] The most recent edition of *Manias, Panics, and Crashes* includes a "report card on the IMF as an international lender of last resort," with a fairly damning verdict: "The Fund has lost sight of its original mandate to manage the international monetary system," and does not adequately recognize the dangers that huge cross-border investment flows* pose to the global economy.[9] The installation of a proper "lender of last resort" seems to be an ongoing project.

Summary

While it does borrow heavily from the ideas of the economist Hyman Minsky,* Kindleberger's *Manias, Panics, and Crashes* was a truly pioneering study that has stood the test of time. If anything, it has grown increasingly relevant to the most pressing, high-stakes questions facing today's economy. The book was published in 1978, when highly rational and mathematical models of efficiency* were all the rage in economics* departments. Rather than follow this trend, *Manias, Panics, and Crashes* provided a novel perspective on how markets work, and one that proved prophetic. Kindleberger used a "literary economics," employing an enjoyable, narrative style to argue that not only is the international economy inherently unstable (due to surges in credit, as Minsky had argued before him in a domestic context), but that the collapse of the US gold standard* and Bretton Woods system* in the 1970s was making it more prone to crisis.

While looking at economic history in an innovative, unorthodox way, the framework Kindleberger developed ultimately anticipated the future. Much more than that, he diagnosed this enduring cycle of mania–panic–crash as a function of credit surges (and, as Aliber later added through further analysis, cross–border investment flows). This conclusion is still debatable, but Kindleberger's detailed and historically substantiated description of the stages of these cycles sheds light on today's global economic events in compelling ways—and makes the ambition of achieving greater international economic stability seem possible. In pursuing this vital aim, *Manias, Panics, and Crashes* remains essential reading.

NOTES

1   Katie Allen, "Why is China's Stock Market in Crisis?" *Guardian*, July 8, 2015, accessed March 22, 2016, http://www.theguardian.com/business/2015/jul/08/china-stock-market-crisis-explained.

2   Will Hutton, "Why Are We Looking on Helplessly as Markets Crash All Over the World?" *Guardian,* January 17, 2016, accessed March 22, 2016, http://www.theguardian.com/commentisfree/2016/jan/17/china-economic-crisis-world-economy-global-capitalism.

3   Andrew Sheng and Xiao Geng, "China's Live Stress Test," Project Syndicate: The World's Opinion Page, July 21, 2015, accessed March 22, 2016, http://www.project-syndicate.org/commentary/china-stock-market-government-intervention-by-andrew-sheng-and-xiao-geng-2015-07?barrier=true.

4   Michael Lewitt, "Oil is Going to Fall by 50%… Again," Michael Lewitt's Sure Money, September 28, 2015, accessed March 22, 2016, http:// suremoneyinvestor.com/2015/09/oil-is-going-to-fall-by-50-again/.

5   Joseph P. Joyce, "The Enduring Relevance of 'Manias, Panics, and Crashes.'" Capital Ebbs and Flows, December 14, 2015, accessed March 22, 2016, https://blogs.wellesley.edu/jjoyce/2015/12/14/the-enduring-relevance-of-manias-panics-and-crashes-2/.

6   Charles P. Kindleberger and Robert Z. Aliber, *Manias, Panics, and Crashes: A History of Financial Crises* (Basingstoke: Palgrave MacMillan, 2015), 35.

7   Kindleberger and Aliber, *Manias, Panics, and Crashes*, 35.

8   Kindleberger and Aliber, *Manias, Panics, and Crashes*, 35.

9   Kindleberger and Aliber, *Manias, Panics and Crashes,* 310–12.

GLOSSARY

GLOSSARY OF TERMS

Asset: a resource or piece of property owned by someone or something, which possesses an economic value.

Bagehot doctrine: in his 1873 book *Lombard Street,* the British businessman and writer Walter Bagehot urged the Bank of England to calm financial panics by lending freely to distressed but solvent banks at a penalty interest rate. This policy became popular among central banks, and was subsequently known as the "Bagehot doctrine."

Balance of payments: a term that describes whether a nation is a creditor or a debtor to the rest of the world.

Behavioral economics: a relatively new field of economics that studies the decision-making processes of individuals and institutions, in an attempt to correct assumptions about their "rational" behavior. The psychological, emotional, and quite irrational aspects of market participants are emphasized in this field.

Behavioral finance: a field of finance exploring the psychological characteristics of market participants to explain market movements and, in particular, irrational systematic errors.

Biologic regularity: a term Kindleberger employs to argue that all financial crises share the same stages and underlying dynamic of boom and bust.

Boom and bust: an economic cycle in which a period of rapid growth and prosperity is suddenly followed by one of sharp economic collapse.

Bretton Woods system: an elaborate postwar agreement between numerous Western countries, establishing monetary arrangements between them as well as other financial relations. It operated from 1945 until the United States abandoned the gold standard in 1971.

Bubble: when the price of an asset, security, or commodity increases significantly in a way that cannot be explained by economic fundamentals.

Capital: financial resources, like cash or the value of other assets, available for use by their owner.

Capitalism: an economic system in which the means of production are privately owned and used in the pursuit of profit. The production of goods and services is based on the laws of supply and demand.

Central bank: a government institution designed to manage the country's interest rate and money supply, among other currency issues.

Classical economics: a movement of the late eighteenth and early nineteenth centuries, largely advocating the creation of free markets.

Contagion: the spread of market disturbances, which can occur regionally, nationally, or internationally. A contagion can either be an economic boom or a crisis that crosses national boundaries.

Credit crunch: an economic situation in which loans or other forms of investment capital are suddenly hard to obtain.

Cross-border investment flows: financial arrangements that cross national borders and typically take the form of loans, acquisitions, or credit.

Currency crisis: a crisis brought on by a fall in the value of a country's currency, which creates instability in its exchange rates with other currencies. This decrease in value and instability can scare off investors. It can also make it difficult for a country to maintain a fixed exchange rate.

Default: the failure to pay a loan or interest on a loan when it is due.

Deflation: a rise in the value of money, and, therefore, a fall in the value of prices.

Displacement: when a significant event like a war, or new policy like deregulation, leads to a sudden boom. Sometimes a displacement occurs when a new technology or innovation radically improves profitability in a market, like the boom in the technological information market of the late 1990s that followed the invention of the Internet.

Dot.com boom: a huge growth in stock prices experienced by industrialized countries in the late 1990s, driven by the growth of technology firms.

East Asian crisis: the 1997 financial crisis that started in Thailand and spread quickly to other East Asian countries.

Economic history: the study of economic phenomena of the past.

Economic nationalism: an ideology in which a nation considers its own economic health to be entirely, and uncompromisingly, paramount at the expense of the global economy's overall health.

Economics: the social science that seeks to describe the production, distribution, and consumption of scarce resources in a world of unlimited wants.

Efficiency: in economics, efficiency is a state in which all resources are optimally allocated—that is, they serve in the best way while minimizing waste.

Efficient market hypothesis (EMH): the idea that asset prices, including stock prices, capture all available information about that asset or respective company.

Federal Reserve: the central bank of the United States, which regulates the nation's monetary and financial systems.

Financial crisis: a broad term applied to various circumstances in which there is a sudden and significant fall in the price of a financial asset or assets.

Financial crisis of 1982: a prolonged crisis when many Latin American countries became unable to service their foreign debt, particularly to US banks, which spread the crisis abroad. The crisis was sparked in the summer of 1982, when Mexico's finance minister informed the US Federal Reserve that Mexico would no longer be able to service its $80 billion in foreign debt. Other South American countries soon followed suit.

Financial crisis of 2008: the worst financial crisis since the Great Depression, featuring widespread bank bailouts, stock market collapses, and housing market busts.

Financial instability hypothesis: an idea developed by the US economist Hyman Minsky, arguing that economic prosperity leads to reckless investment behavior, fueled by credit.

Financial regulation: the supervision of financial institutions, typically by government agencies and through prescribed requirements and guidelines.

Fixed exchange rates: when a currency's value is pegged to the value of another currency, or to a basket of currencies, by the government. Sometimes an exchange rate is fixed by declaring it to be worth a certain quantity of gold.

Free-floating exchange rates: when a currency is not fixed by its government, but instead allowed to fluctuate on the global currency markets.

Global economy: the interdependence of national economies around the world in trade and industry, functioning as one economic system.

Gold standard: when a country declares that its currency is worth a certain amount of gold, thereby fixing the value of the currency.

Great Depression: an extremely long and deep economic depression that began in 1929 and lasted until World War II.

Hegemony: a predominant position of leadership, or a predominant sphere of influence, held by one country over others.

Inflation: a fall in the value of money, and a rise in prices. This is often brought on by an increase in the money supply.

Interest rates: the price of borrowing, typically expressed as an annual percentage of the loan outstanding.

International balance of payments: the statement of a nation's economic transactions with the rest of the world. Each country tends to be a persistent "debtor" or "creditor" nation.

International Monetary Fund (IMF): an institution, based in the United States, founded to secure international financial stability and cooperation; it commonly lends money to nations in financial distress in return for structural changes to their economies, such as spending cuts and the privatization of state-owned businesses and assets.

International propagation: an idea developed by Kindleberger, which held that due to the interdependence of the global economy, financial crises can spread from one country to another, as if through "contagion."

Investor: a person who provides capital in the hope of gaining a financial return in the future. Such capital can be provided in the form of equity, debt securities, real estate, commodities, and so on.

Japanese credit crisis: a major financial crisis in Japan in the 1980s, which saw a boom-and-bust scenario in stocks and real estate.

Lehman Brothers: a large international investment bank that went bankrupt in September 2008, triggering a worldwide financial crisis.

Lender of last resort: a central bank that loans money to other banks or similar financial institutions that are nearing insolvency and collapse.

Marshall Plan: officially known as the European Recovery Program, the Marshall Plan was a post–World War II economic support package provided to Western Europe by the United States. It was worth $13 billion.

Minsky Model: the economist Hyman Minsky's model of the credit cycle, which Kindleberger developed further. The model has five stages: displacement, boom, euphoria, profit-taking, and panic.

Monetarism: a school of thought within economics based on the belief that an economy's performance is most strongly influenced by changes in the money supply.

Nationalism: is an extreme form of patriotism, which typically includes the belief that the interests of one's own nation-state are superior to those of other countries.

Negative feedback loop: when the disruption from an established norm creates a response that amplifies the negative change.

Nobel Prize: a set of international awards given every year to recognize outstanding academic, cultural, or scientific achievements.

Oil shock: an unexpected, dramatic rise in the price of oil that reverberates throughout an economy, often causing overall inflation to rise sharply as well.

Payment imbalance: when a nation exports more than it imports, or vice versa.

Peso devaluation: in December 1994, the Mexican government devalued its peso against the US dollar by almost 15 percent. Among the unexpected consequences was a mass sell-off of Mexican assets by international investors wanting to remove their money from the country. This prompted a financial crisis that soon spread to Asia and other parts of Latin America.

Positive feedback loops: when the disruption from an established norm creates a response that amplifies the positive change.

Pro-cyclical: expresses the idea that credit cycles are self-perpetuating. So increases in the supply of credit prolong the expansion of a boom, and decreases in the supply of credit intensify the subsequent crash.

Psychology: the study of the human mind and behavior.

Securities: a financial agreement signifying ownership in a public-traded corporation (like a stock), a creditor relationship (bond) or right to ownership (option).

South Sea bubble: one of the greatest financial bubbles in history, associated with the collapse in value of shares in the South Sea Company—a British public-private company founded in 1711 that was granted a monopoly to trade with South America. Prices of shares in the company rose to astronomical heights before crashing dramatically in 1720.

Speculator: someone who invests in a financial asset hoping for a short-term gain over the next few days or weeks.

State Department: the US federal government's ministry for dealing with America's international relations.

Stock: a security that provides a share of ownership in a corporation, and so a claim on future assets and earnings of that business.

Stock market crash of 1987: also known as "Black Monday," this was a crash that occurred on 19 October, 1987, occasioned by tension in the Persian Gulf, when the Dow Jones Industrial Average fell over 20 percent. Other stock markets around the world experienced huge losses on the same date.

Trade surplus: when a country exports more to the rest of the world than it imports.

World War I: also known as the Great War, this was a global war from 1914 to 1918 which took place between the "Allies" (Great Britain, France, the Russian Empire, and the United States), and the "Central Powers" of Germany and Austro-Hungary.

World War II: a global war lasting 1939–45, primarily between the "Allies" (which included the United States, Soviet Union, Great Britain, and France), and the "Axis" powers of Germany, Italy, and Japan.

PEOPLE MENTIONED IN THE TEXT

Robert Z. Aliber (b. 1930) is a professor emeritus of economics at the University of Chicago. His primary subject has been the nature of foreign direct investment. Since Kindleberger's death, Aliber has edited and updated *Manias, Panics, and Crashes* through its last three editions.

Walter Bagehot (1826–77) was a British businessman, journalist, and political commentator. He wrote extensively about economics and the nature of financial crisis.

Gordon Brown (b. 1951) was prime minister of the United Kingdom from 2007 to 2010, and chancellor of the exchequer from 1997 to 2007.

Michel Chevalier (1806–79) was a French economist and statesman who commentated extensively on the nature of markets and market instability.

Charles Darwin (1809–82) was an English naturalist and scientist, best known for his book *The Origin of Species* (1859), the text on which modern evolutionary theory is largely founded.

Barry Eichengreen (b. 1952) is an American economist and academic.

Eugene F. Fama (b. 1939) is a Nobel Prize–winning economist whose primary subject has been the analysis of stock market behavior. He is credited with making the efficient market hypothesis credible through empirical evidence.

Milton Friedman (1912–2006) was a professor in economics and political science at the University of California, Berkeley. His work looks at the international monetary and financial system.

John Kenneth Galbraith (1908–2006) was a distinguished economist and public intellectual who taught at Harvard for over 50 years.

Timothy F. Geithner (b. 1961) is a former economic policymaker who served as United States secretary of the treasury from 2009 to 2013.

Robert Gilpin (b. 1930) is professor emeritus of politics and international affairs at Princeton University. His work focuses on the international aspects of political economy.

Daniel Kahneman (b. 1934) is professor emeritus of psychology and public affairs at Princeton University. He researched empirical data (data verifiable by observation) to challenge the view of "rational" decision-making so popular in economic theory, making him an esteemed figure within behavioral economics.

Robert Keohane (b. 1941) is a professor of political science at Princeton University. His work built upon that of Charles P. Kindleberger, leading to new ideas about "hegemonic stability."

John Maynard Keynes (1883–1946) was an English economist whose macroeconomic theories radically changed the subject and formed the basis for today's "Keynesian school" of economics.

Paul Krugman (b. 1953) is an American Nobel Prize–winning economist whose primary subject has been international trade and the geographic distribution of economic activity.

Burton G. Malkiel (b. 1932) is an American academic, investor, and writer. He is the author of *A Random Walk Down Wall Street* (1973) and an emeritus professor at Princeton University.

Alfred Marshall (1842–1924) was a distinguished British economist and is credited as one of the founders of neoclassic economics.

John Maudlin is a financier, economist, author, and online commentator on the subject of financial markets and economic history.

Lawrence G. McDonald is the author of *A Colossal Failure of Common Sense: The Inside Story of the Collapse of Lehman Brothers* (2009), which details the collapse of the Lehman Brothers bank from an insider's perspective. McDonald had been a vice-president of the bank.

John Stuart Mill (1806–73) was an English economist and a notable philosopher. He made wide-ranging contributions to economics, political theory, and social theory.

Patrick Minford (b. 1943) is a British economist, and professor of applied economics at Cardiff University.

Hyman Minsky (1919–96) was a professor of economics at Washington University in St. Louis. His work focused on the nature of financial crises.

Chuck Prince (b. 1950) is an American businessman, and the former chairman and chief executive of the multinational finance corporation Citigroup.

Robert J. Shiller (b. 1946) is a Nobel Prize–winning economist and author of *Irrational Exuberance* (2000). His work in financial economics and behavioral finance is skeptical of the efficient market hypothesis.

Robert Skidelsky (b. 1939) is a British economic historian and emeritus professor of political economy at the University of Warwick.

Adam Smith (1723–90) was a Scottish economist and philosopher who played a key role in the Scottish Enlightenment. His book *The Wealth of Nations* (1776) is often considered a founding work in the subject of economics.

Robert M. Solow (b. 1924) is a Nobel Prize–winning economist and emeritus Institute Professor in the economics department of Massachusetts Institute of Technology (MIT). He is best-known for his work on economic growth.

George Soros (b. 1930) is one of the world's wealthiest and most famous investors. He is chairman of Soros Fund Management and an open skeptic of the efficient market hypothesis.

Lawrence Summers (b. 1954) is an American economist who was US secretary of the treasury from 1999 to 2001. He was also chief economist at the World Bank from 1991 to 1993.

Nassim Nicholas Taleb (b. 1960) is a Lebanese American author and investor. His work on the nature of randomness and uncertainty has had an impact on the worlds of finance and philosophy, among other disciplines.

Jonathan Tepper is an American economist, author, and founder of Variant Perception, a macroeconomic research group.

Amos Tversky (1937–96) was a cognitive and mathematical psychologist. His most famous work connected the way the human mind handles risk to cognitive bias (which means interpreting information in a way that confirms preexisting prejudices).

Vicky Ward (b. 1969) is a British journalist and the author of *The Devil's Casino: Friendship, Betrayal, and the High Stakes Games Played Inside Lehman Brothers* (2010), which detailed the collapse of the investment bank.

WORKS CITED

WORKS CITED

Allen, Katie. "Why is China's Stock Market in Crisis?" *Guardian*. July 8, 2015. Accessed March 21, 2016. http://www.theguardian.com/business/2015/jul/08/china-stock-market-crisis-explained.

W. Ashworth. "*Manias, Panics, and Crashes: A History of Financial Crises* by Charles P. Kindleberger." *Economic History Review* 32, no. 3 (August, 1979): 421–2.

Babkar, Mamta. "Soros: The Efficient Market Hypothesis Has Run Into Bankruptcy." *Business Insider*. Accessed March 21, 2016. http://www.businessinsider.com/financial-advisor-insights-june-26-2013-6?IR=T.

Buttonwood. "China's Stockmarket: The Great Leap Backward." *Economist*. Accessed March 21, 2016. http://www.economist.com/blogs/buttonwood/2015/07/chinas-stockmarket.

Chevalier, Michel. *Lettres sur l'Amérique du Nord*. Brussels: Société belge du librairie, 1838.

Clark, Peter, Natalia Tamirisa, and Shang-Jin Wei, with Azim Sadikov, and Li Zeng. "Exchange Rate Volatility and Trade Flows – Some New Evidence." International Monetary Fund, May 2004. Accessed March 21, 2016. https://www.imf.org/external/np/res/exrate/2004/eng/051904.pdf.

Cooper, Richard, Barry Eichengreen, Gerald Holtham, Robert Putnam and Randall Henning. *Can Nations Agree? Issues in International Economic Cooperation*. Washington, DC: Brookings Institution Press, 1989.

Economist. "Of Manias, Panics, and Crashes." July 17, 2003. Accessed March 21, 2016. http://www.economist.com/node/1923462.

Fosler, Gail. "Lessons from Kindleberger on the Financial Crisis." *The Gail Fosler Group*. April 28, 2013. Accessed March 21, 2016. http://www.gailfosler.com/lessons-from-kindleberger-on-the-financial-crisis.

Geithner, Timothy F. "Change and Challenges Facing the US Financial System." New York Bankers Association's Annual Financial Services Forum, *BIS Review* 18 (March, 2004).

_____. *Stress Test: Reflections on Financial Crises*. New York: Crown Publishers, 2014.

Gekas, Sakis. "Different Because Worse." *Dublin Review of Books* 16 (Winter 2010). Accessed March 21, 2016. http://www.drb.ie/essays/different-because-worse.

Gilpin, Robert. *The Political Economy of International Relations*. Princeton: Princeton University Press, 1987.

Hakes, David R., and David C. Rose. "The 1979–1982 Monetary Policy Experiment: Monetarist, Anti-Monetarist, or Quasi-Monetarist?" *Journal of Post Keynesian Economics* 15, no. 2 (Winter 1992–3): 281–8.

Hutton, Will. "Why are we looking on helplessly as markets crash all over the world?" *Guardian*, January 17, 2016. Accessed March 21, 2016. http://www. theguardian.com/commentisfree/2016/jan/17/china-economic-crisis-world-economy-global-capitalism.

Ishikawa, Tetsuya. *How I Caused the Credit Crunch: An Insider's Story of the Financial Meltdown*. London: Icon Books, 2009.

Joyce, Joseph P. "The Enduring Relevance of 'Manias, Panics, and Crashes.'" *Capital Ebbs and Flows*. Accessed March 21, 2016. https://blogs.wellesley.edu/ jjoyce/2015/12/14/the-enduring-relevance-of-manias-panics-and-crashes-2/.

Keohane, Robert. *After Hegemony: Cooperation and Discord in the World of Political Economy.* Princeton: Princeton University Press, 1984.

Kindleberger, Charles P. *The Dollar Shortage*. New York: John Wiley & Sons, 1950.

_____. *International Short-term Capital Movements*. New York: Columbia University Press, 1937.

_____. *The World in Depression, 1929–1939*. Berkeley; Los Angeles: University of California Press, 1973.

_____. *The World in Depression, 1929–1939.* Edited by J. Bradford DeLong and Barry Eichengreen. Berkeley: University of California Press, 2013.

Kindleberger. Charles P., and Robert Z. Aliber. *Manias, Panics, and Crashes: A History of Financial Crises*. London: Palgrave MacMillan, 2015.

Kirkup, James. "Gordon Brown admits he was wrong to claim he had ended 'boom and bust.'" *Telegraph*, November 21, 2008. Accessed March 21, 2016. http://www.telegraph.co.uk/finance/recession/3497533/Gordon-Brown-admits-he-was-wrong-to-claim-he-had-ended-boom-and-bust.html

Knoop, Todd A. *Business Cycle Economics: Understanding Recessions and Depressions from Boom to Bust*. Santa Barbara, CA: Praeger, 2015.

Kobrak, Christopher and Mira Wilkins, ed. *History and Financial Crisis: Lessons from the 20th Century.* New York: Routledge, 2013.

Krugman, Paul and Robin Wells. "The Busts Keep Getting Bigger: Why?" *New York Review of Books*, July 14, 2011. Accessed March 21, 2016. http://www. nybooks.com/articles/2011/07/14/busts-keep-getting-bigger-why/

Krugman, Paul. "China Bites the Cherry." *New York Times*, August 12, 2015. Accessed March 21, 2016. http://krugman.blogs.nytimes.com/2015/08/12/china-bites-the-cherry/?_r=0.

_____. "Why We Regulate." *New York Times*, May 13, 2012. Accessed March 21, 2016. http://www.nytimes.com/2012/05/14/opinion/krugman-why-we-regulate.html.

Lewitt, Michael. "Oil is Going to Fall by 50%... Again." Michael Lewitt's Sure Money, September 28, 2015. Accessed on January 17, 2016. http://suremoneyinvestor.com/2015/09/oil-is-going-to-fall-by-50-again/.

McDonald, Lawrence G., with Patrick Robinson. *A Colossal Failure of Common Sense: The Inside Story of the Collapse of Lehman Brothers*. New York: Three Rivers Press, 2009.

Malkiel, Burton G. "The Efficient Market Hypothesis and Its Critics." *Journal of Economic Perspectives,* 17, no. 1 (Winter, 2003): 59–82.

_____. *A Random Walk Down Wall Street: The Time-Tested Strategy for Successful Investing.* New York: W.W. Norton & Company, 2015.

Maudlin, John and Jonathan Tepper. *Code Red: How to Protect Your Savings From the Coming Crisis.* Hoboken: John Wiley & Sons, 2013.

Meardon, Stephen. "On Kindleberger and Hegemony: From Berlin to M.I.T. and Back." Bowdoin Digital Commons, September 29, 2013. Accessed March 21, 2016. http://digitalcommons.bowdoin.edu/cgi/viewcontent.cgi?article=1003&context=econpapers.

Minford, Patrick. "*Manias, Panics, and Crashes. A History of Financial Crises*. By Charles P. Kindleberger." *Economic Journal* 89 (December, 1979).

Mody, Ashoka. "Germany must lead by example on fixing its banks." *Financial Times*, May 27, 2013. Accessed March 21, 2016. http://www.ft.com/intl/cms/s/0/10e7ccbe-c46f-11e2-9ac0-00144feab7de.html#axzz43Y4Huy4b.

Murray, Nick. "A Treasure Trove of Financial Folly." *Financial Advisor*, January 1, 2016. Accessed March 24, 2016. http://www.fa-mag.com/news/a-treasure-trove-of-financial-folly-24440.html.

Pasotti, Piero and Alessandro Vercelli. "Kindleberger and Financial Crises." *Financialisation, Economy, Society, and Sustainable Development Working Paper Series* 104, February 2015. Accessed March 21, 2016. http://fessud.eu/wp-content/uploads/2015/01/Kindleberger-and-Financial-Crises-Fessud-final_Working-Paper-104.pdf.

Patterson, Scott. *The Quants: How a New Breed of Math Whizzes Conquered Wall Street and Nearly Destroyed It.* New York: Crown Business, 2010.

Sheng, Andres and Xiao Geng. "China's Live Stress Test." *Project Syndicate: The World's Opinion Page*. July 21, 2015. Accessed March 21, 2016. http://www.project-syndicate.org/commentary/china-stock-market-government-intervention-by-andrew-sheng-and-xiao-geng-2015-07?barrier=true.

Shiller, Robert J. *Irrational Exuberance*. Princeton: Princeton University Press, 2015.

Sylla, Richard. "Financial Disturbances and Depressions: The View from Economic History." Social Science Research Network: Levy Economics Institute Working Paper 47 (April, 1991).

Taleb, Nassim Nicholas. *The Black Swan: The Impact of the Highly Improbable*. London: Penguin, 2007.

Turk, Michael H. *The Idea of History in Constructing Economics*. Abingdon: Routledge, 2016.

Ward, Vicky. *The Devil's Casino: Friendship, Betrayal, and the High-Stakes Games Played Inside Lehman Brothers*. Hoboken: John Wiley & Sons, 2010.

Westbrook, David. *City of Gold: An Apology for Global Capitalism in a Time of Discontent*. New York: Routledge, 2004.

Zweig, Jason. "Read It and Reap: The Best Books for Investors." *Wall Street Journal*. November 28, 2015. Accessed March 21, 2016. http://www.wsj.com/articles/read-it-and-reap-the-best-books-for-investors-1417213387.

THE MACAT LIBRARY
BY DISCIPLINE

AFRICANA STUDIES

Chinua Achebe's *An Image of Africa: Racism in Conrad's Heart of Darkness*
W. E. B. Du Bois's *The Souls of Black Folk*
Zora Neale Huston's *Characteristics of Negro Expression*
Martin Luther King Jr's *Why We Can't Wait*
Toni Morrison's *Playing in the Dark: Whiteness in the American Literary Imagination*

ANTHROPOLOGY

Arjun Appadurai's *Modernity at Large: Cultural Dimensions of Globalisation*
Philippe Ariès's *Centuries of Childhood*
Franz Boas's *Race, Language and Culture*
Kim Chan & Renée Mauborgne's *Blue Ocean Strategy*
Jared Diamond's *Guns, Germs & Steel: the Fate of Human Societies*
Jared Diamond's *Collapse: How Societies Choose to Fail or Survive*
E. E. Evans-Pritchard's *Witchcraft, Oracles and Magic Among the Azande*
James Ferguson's *The Anti-Politics Machine*
Clifford Geertz's *The Interpretation of Cultures*
David Graeber's *Debt: the First 5000 Years*
Karen Ho's *Liquidated: An Ethnography of Wall Street*
Geert Hofstede's *Culture's Consequences: Comparing Values, Behaviors, Institutes and Organizations across Nations*
Claude Lévi-Strauss's *Structural Anthropology*
Jay Macleod's *Ain't No Makin' It: Aspirations and Attainment in a Low-Income Neighborhood*
Saba Mahmood's *The Politics of Piety: The Islamic Revival and the Feminist Subject*
Marcel Mauss's *The Gift*

BUSINESS

Jean Lave & Etienne Wenger's *Situated Learning*
Theodore Levitt's *Marketing Myopia*
Burton G. Malkiel's *A Random Walk Down Wall Street*
Douglas McGregor's *The Human Side of Enterprise*
Michael Porter's *Competitive Strategy: Creating and Sustaining Superior Performance*
John Kotter's *Leading Change*
C. K. Prahalad & Gary Hamel's *The Core Competence of the Corporation*

CRIMINOLOGY

Michelle Alexander's *The New Jim Crow: Mass Incarceration in the Age of Colorblindness*
Michael R. Gottfredson & Travis Hirschi's *A General Theory of Crime*
Richard Herrnstein & Charles A. Murray's *The Bell Curve: Intelligence and Class Structure in American Life*
Elizabeth Loftus's *Eyewitness Testimony*
Jay Macleod's *Ain't No Makin' It: Aspirations and Attainment in a Low-Income Neighborhood*
Philip Zimbardo's *The Lucifer Effect*

ECONOMICS

Janet Abu-Lughod's *Before European Hegemony*
Ha-Joon Chang's *Kicking Away the Ladder*
David Brion Davis's *The Problem of Slavery in the Age of Revolution*
Milton Friedman's *The Role of Monetary Policy*
Milton Friedman's *Capitalism and Freedom*
David Graeber's *Debt: the First 5000 Years*
Friedrich Hayek's *The Road to Serfdom*
Karen Ho's *Liquidated: An Ethnography of Wall Street*

John Maynard Keynes's *The General Theory of Employment, Interest and Money*
Charles P. Kindleberger's *Manias, Panics and Crashes*
Robert Lucas's *Why Doesn't Capital Flow from Rich to Poor Countries?*
Burton G. Malkiel's *A Random Walk Down Wall Street*
Thomas Robert Malthus's *An Essay on the Principle of Population*
Karl Marx's *Capital*
Thomas Piketty's *Capital in the Twenty-First Century*
Amartya Sen's *Development as Freedom*
Adam Smith's *The Wealth of Nations*
Nassim Nicholas Taleb's *The Black Swan: The Impact of the Highly Improbable*
Amos Tversky's & Daniel Kahneman's *Judgment under Uncertainty: Heuristics and Biases*
Mahbub Ul Haq's *Reflections on Human Development*
Max Weber's *The Protestant Ethic and the Spirit of Capitalism*

FEMINISM AND GENDER STUDIES

Judith Butler's *Gender Trouble*
Simone De Beauvoir's *The Second Sex*
Michel Foucault's *History of Sexuality*
Betty Friedan's *The Feminine Mystique*
Saba Mahmood's *The Politics of Piety: The Islamic Revival and the Feminist Subject*
Joan Wallach Scott's *Gender and the Politics of History*
Mary Wollstonecraft's *A Vindication of the Rights of Woman*
Virginia Woolf's *A Room of One's Own*

GEOGRAPHY

The Brundtland Report's *Our Common Future*
Rachel Carson's *Silent Spring*
Charles Darwin's *On the Origin of Species*
James Ferguson's *The Anti-Politics Machine*
Jane Jacobs's *The Death and Life of Great American Cities*
James Lovelock's *Gaia: A New Look at Life on Earth*
Amartya Sen's *Development as Freedom*
Mathis Wackernagel & William Rees's *Our Ecological Footprint*

HISTORY

Janet Abu-Lughod's *Before European Hegemony*
Benedict Anderson's *Imagined Communities*
Bernard Bailyn's *The Ideological Origins of the American Revolution*
Hanna Batatu's *The Old Social Classes And The Revolutionary Movements Of Iraq*
Christopher Browning's *Ordinary Men: Reserve Police Batallion 101 and the Final Solution in Poland*
Edmund Burke's *Reflections on the Revolution in France*
William Cronon's *Nature's Metropolis: Chicago And The Great West*
Alfred W. Crosby's *The Columbian Exchange*
Hamid Dabashi's *Iran: A People Interrupted*
David Brion Davis's *The Problem of Slavery in the Age of Revolution*
Nathalie Zemon Davis's *The Return of Martin Guerre*
Jared Diamond's *Guns, Germs & Steel: the Fate of Human Societies*
Frank Dikotter's *Mao's Great Famine*
John W Dower's *War Without Mercy: Race And Power In The Pacific War*
W. E. B. Du Bois's *The Souls of Black Folk*
Richard J. Evans's *In Defence of History*
Lucien Febvre's *The Problem of Unbelief in the 16th Century*
Sheila Fitzpatrick's *Everyday Stalinism*

Eric Foner's *Reconstruction: America's Unfinished Revolution, 1863-1877*
Michel Foucault's *Discipline and Punish*
Michel Foucault's *History of Sexuality*
Francis Fukuyama's *The End of History and the Last Man*
John Lewis Gaddis's *We Now Know: Rethinking Cold War History*
Ernest Gellner's *Nations and Nationalism*
Eugene Genovese's *Roll, Jordan, Roll: The World the Slaves Made*
Carlo Ginzburg's *The Night Battles*
Daniel Goldhagen's *Hitler's Willing Executioners*
Jack Goldstone's *Revolution and Rebellion in the Early Modern World*
Antonio Gramsci's *The Prison Notebooks*
Alexander Hamilton, John Jay & James Madison's *The Federalist Papers*
Christopher Hill's *The World Turned Upside Down*
Carole Hillenbrand's *The Crusades: Islamic Perspectives*
Thomas Hobbes's *Leviathan*
Eric Hobsbawm's *The Age Of Revolution*
John A. Hobson's *Imperialism: A Study*
Albert Hourani's *History of the Arab Peoples*
Samuel P. Huntington's *The Clash of Civilizations and the Remaking of World Order*
C. L. R. James's *The Black Jacobins*
Tony Judt's *Postwar: A History of Europe Since 1945*
Ernst Kantorowicz's *The King's Two Bodies: A Study in Medieval Political Theology*
Paul Kennedy's *The Rise and Fall of the Great Powers*
Ian Kershaw's *The "Hitler Myth": Image and Reality in the Third Reich*
John Maynard Keynes's *The General Theory of Employment, Interest and Money*
Charles P. Kindleberger's *Manias, Panics and Crashes*
Martin Luther King Jr's *Why We Can't Wait*
Henry Kissinger's *World Order: Reflections on the Character of Nations and the Course of History*
Thomas Kuhn's *The Structure of Scientific Revolutions*
Georges Lefebvre's *The Coming of the French Revolution*
John Locke's *Two Treatises of Government*
Niccolò Machiavelli's *The Prince*
Thomas Robert Malthus's *An Essay on the Principle of Population*
Mahmood Mamdani's *Citizen and Subject: Contemporary Africa And The Legacy Of Late Colonialism*
Karl Marx's *Capital*
Stanley Milgram's *Obedience to Authority*
John Stuart Mill's *On Liberty*
Thomas Paine's *Common Sense*
Thomas Paine's *Rights of Man*
Geoffrey Parker's *Global Crisis: War, Climate Change and Catastrophe in the Seventeenth Century*
Jonathan Riley-Smith's *The First Crusade and the Idea of Crusading*
Jean-Jacques Rousseau's *The Social Contract*
Joan Wallach Scott's *Gender and the Politics of History*
Theda Skocpol's *States and Social Revolutions*
Adam Smith's *The Wealth of Nations*
Timothy Snyder's *Bloodlands: Europe Between Hitler and Stalin*
Sun Tzu's *The Art of War*
Keith Thomas's *Religion and the Decline of Magic*
Thucydides's *The History of the Peloponnesian War*
Frederick Jackson Turner's *The Significance of the Frontier in American History*
Odd Arne Westad's *The Global Cold War: Third World Interventions And The Making Of Our Times*

LITERATURE

Chinua Achebe's *An Image of Africa: Racism in Conrad's Heart of Darkness*
Roland Barthes's *Mythologies*
Homi K. Bhabha's *The Location of Culture*
Judith Butler's *Gender Trouble*
Simone De Beauvoir's *The Second Sex*
Ferdinand De Saussure's *Course in General Linguistics*
T. S. Eliot's *The Sacred Wood: Essays on Poetry and Criticism*
Zora Neale Huston's *Characteristics of Negro Expression*
Toni Morrison's *Playing in the Dark: Whiteness in the American Literary Imagination*
Edward Said's *Orientalism*
Gayatri Chakravorty Spivak's *Can the Subaltern Speak?*
Mary Wollstonecraft's *A Vindication of the Rights of Women*
Virginia Woolf's *A Room of One's Own*

PHILOSOPHY

Elizabeth Anscombe's *Modern Moral Philosophy*
Hannah Arendt's *The Human Condition*
Aristotle's *Metaphysics*
Aristotle's *Nicomachean Ethics*
Edmund Gettier's *Is Justified True Belief Knowledge?*
Georg Wilhelm Friedrich Hegel's *Phenomenology of Spirit*
David Hume's *Dialogues Concerning Natural Religion*
David Hume's *The Enquiry for Human Understanding*
Immanuel Kant's *Religion within the Boundaries of Mere Reason*
Immanuel Kant's *Critique of Pure Reason*
Søren Kierkegaard's *The Sickness Unto Death*
Søren Kierkegaard's *Fear and Trembling*
C. S. Lewis's *The Abolition of Man*
Alasdair MacIntyre's *After Virtue*
Marcus Aurelius's *Meditations*
Friedrich Nietzsche's *On the Genealogy of Morality*
Friedrich Nietzsche's *Beyond Good and Evil*
Plato's *Republic*
Plato's *Symposium*
Jean-Jacques Rousseau's *The Social Contract*
Gilbert Ryle's *The Concept of Mind*
Baruch Spinoza's *Ethics*
Sun Tzu's *The Art of War*
Ludwig Wittgenstein's *Philosophical Investigations*

POLITICS

Benedict Anderson's *Imagined Communities*
Aristotle's *Politics*
Bernard Bailyn's *The Ideological Origins of the American Revolution*
Edmund Burke's *Reflections on the Revolution in France*
John C. Calhoun's *A Disquisition on Government*
Ha-Joon Chang's *Kicking Away the Ladder*
Hamid Dabashi's *Iran: A People Interrupted*
Hamid Dabashi's *Theology of Discontent: The Ideological Foundation of the Islamic Revolution in Iran*
Robert Dahl's *Democracy and its Critics*
Robert Dahl's *Who Governs?*
David Brion Davis's *The Problem of Slavery in the Age of Revolution*

Alexis De Tocqueville's *Democracy in America*
James Ferguson's *The Anti-Politics Machine*
Frank Dikotter's *Mao's Great Famine*
Sheila Fitzpatrick's *Everyday Stalinism*
Eric Foner's *Reconstruction: America's Unfinished Revolution, 1863-1877*
Milton Friedman's *Capitalism and Freedom*
Francis Fukuyama's *The End of History and the Last Man*
John Lewis Gaddis's *We Now Know: Rethinking Cold War History*
Ernest Gellner's *Nations and Nationalism*
David Graeber's *Debt: the First 5000 Years*
Antonio Gramsci's *The Prison Notebooks*
Alexander Hamilton, John Jay & James Madison's *The Federalist Papers*
Friedrich Hayek's *The Road to Serfdom*
Christopher Hill's *The World Turned Upside Down*
Thomas Hobbes's *Leviathan*
John A. Hobson's *Imperialism: A Study*
Samuel P. Huntington's *The Clash of Civilizations and the Remaking of World Order*
Tony Judt's *Postwar: A History of Europe Since 1945*
David C. Kang's *China Rising: Peace, Power and Order in East Asia*
Paul Kennedy's *The Rise and Fall of Great Powers*
Robert Keohane's *After Hegemony*
Martin Luther King Jr.'s *Why We Can't Wait*
Henry Kissinger's *World Order: Reflections on the Character of Nations and the Course of History*
John Locke's *Two Treatises of Government*
Niccolò Machiavelli's *The Prince*
Thomas Robert Malthus's *An Essay on the Principle of Population*
Mahmood Mamdani's *Citizen and Subject: Contemporary Africa And The Legacy Of Late Colonialism*
Karl Marx's *Capital*
John Stuart Mill's *On Liberty*
John Stuart Mill's *Utilitarianism*
Hans Morgenthau's *Politics Among Nations*
Thomas Paine's *Common Sense*
Thomas Paine's *Rights of Man*
Thomas Piketty's *Capital in the Twenty-First Century*
Robert D. Putman's *Bowling Alone*
John Rawls's *Theory of Justice*
Jean-Jacques Rousseau's *The Social Contract*
Theda Skocpol's *States and Social Revolutions*
Adam Smith's *The Wealth of Nations*
Sun Tzu's *The Art of War*
Henry David Thoreau's *Civil Disobedience*
Thucydides's *The History of the Peloponnesian War*
Kenneth Waltz's *Theory of International Politics*
Max Weber's *Politics as a Vocation*
Odd Arne Westad's *The Global Cold War: Third World Interventions And The Making Of Our Times*

POSTCOLONIAL STUDIES

Roland Barthes's *Mythologies*
Frantz Fanon's *Black Skin, White Masks*
Homi K. Bhabha's *The Location of Culture*
Gustavo Gutiérrez's *A Theology of Liberation*
Edward Said's *Orientalism*
Gayatri Chakravorty Spivak's *Can the Subaltern Speak?*

PSYCHOLOGY

Gordon Allport's *The Nature of Prejudice*
Alan Baddeley & Graham Hitch's *Aggression: A Social Learning Analysis*
Albert Bandura's *Aggression: A Social Learning Analysis*
Leon Festinger's *A Theory of Cognitive Dissonance*
Sigmund Freud's *The Interpretation of Dreams*
Betty Friedan's *The Feminine Mystique*
Michael R. Gottfredson & Travis Hirschi's *A General Theory of Crime*
Eric Hoffer's *The True Believer: Thoughts on the Nature of Mass Movements*
William James's *Principles of Psychology*
Elizabeth Loftus's *Eyewitness Testimony*
A. H. Maslow's *A Theory of Human Motivation*
Stanley Milgram's *Obedience to Authority*
Steven Pinker's *The Better Angels of Our Nature*
Oliver Sacks's *The Man Who Mistook His Wife For a Hat*
Richard Thaler & Cass Sunstein's *Nudge: Improving Decisions About Health, Wealth and Happiness*
Amos Tversky's *Judgment under Uncertainty: Heuristics and Biases*
Philip Zimbardo's *The Lucifer Effect*

SCIENCE

Rachel Carson's *Silent Spring*
William Cronon's *Nature's Metropolis: Chicago And The Great West*
Alfred W. Crosby's *The Columbian Exchange*
Charles Darwin's *On the Origin of Species*
Richard Dawkin's *The Selfish Gene*
Thomas Kuhn's *The Structure of Scientific Revolutions*
Geoffrey Parker's *Global Crisis: War, Climate Change and Catastrophe in the Seventeenth Century*
Mathis Wackernagel & William Rees's *Our Ecological Footprint*

SOCIOLOGY

Michelle Alexander's *The New Jim Crow: Mass Incarceration in the Age of Colorblindness*
Gordon Allport's *The Nature of Prejudice*
Albert Bandura's *Aggression: A Social Learning Analysis*
Hanna Batatu's *The Old Social Classes And The Revolutionary Movements Of Iraq*
Ha-Joon Chang's *Kicking Away the Ladder*
W. E. B. Du Bois's *The Souls of Black Folk*
Émile Durkheim's *On Suicide*
Frantz Fanon's *Black Skin, White Masks*
Frantz Fanon's *The Wretched of the Earth*
Eric Foner's *Reconstruction: America's Unfinished Revolution, 1863-1877*
Eugene Genovese's *Roll, Jordan, Roll: The World the Slaves Made*
Jack Goldstone's *Revolution and Rebellion in the Early Modern World*
Antonio Gramsci's *The Prison Notebooks*
Richard Herrnstein & Charles A Murray's *The Bell Curve: Intelligence and Class Structure in American Life*
Eric Hoffer's *The True Believer: Thoughts on the Nature of Mass Movements*
Jane Jacobs's *The Death and Life of Great American Cities*
Robert Lucas's *Why Doesn't Capital Flow from Rich to Poor Countries?*
Jay Macleod's *Ain't No Makin' It: Aspirations and Attainment in a Low Income Neighborhood*
Elaine May's *Homeward Bound: American Families in the Cold War Era*
Douglas McGregor's *The Human Side of Enterprise*
C. Wright Mills's *The Sociological Imagination*

The Macat Library By Discipline

Thomas Piketty's *Capital in the Twenty-First Century*
Robert D. Putman's *Bowling Alone*
David Riesman's *The Lonely Crowd: A Study of the Changing American Character*
Edward Said's *Orientalism*
Joan Wallach Scott's *Gender and the Politics of History*
Theda Skocpol's *States and Social Revolutions*
Max Weber's *The Protestant Ethic and the Spirit of Capitalism*

THEOLOGY

Augustine's *Confessions*
Benedict's *Rule of St Benedict*
Gustavo Gutiérrez's *A Theology of Liberation*
Carole Hillenbrand's *The Crusades: Islamic Perspectives*
David Hume's *Dialogues Concerning Natural Religion*
Immanuel Kant's *Religion within the Boundaries of Mere Reason*
Ernst Kantorowicz's *The King's Two Bodies: A Study in Medieval Political Theology*
Søren Kierkegaard's *The Sickness Unto Death*
C. S. Lewis's *The Abolition of Man*
Saba Mahmood's *The Politics of Piety: The Islamic Revival and the Feminist Subject*
Baruch Spinoza's *Ethics*
Keith Thomas's *Religion and the Decline of Magic*

COMING SOON

Chris Argyris's *The Individual and the Organisation*
Seyla Benhabib's *The Rights of Others*
Walter Benjamin's *The Work Of Art in the Age of Mechanical Reproduction*
John Berger's *Ways of Seeing*
Pierre Bourdieu's *Outline of a Theory of Practice*
Mary Douglas's *Purity and Danger*
Roland Dworkin's *Taking Rights Seriously*
James G. March's *Exploration and Exploitation in Organisational Learning*
Ikujiro Nonaka's *A Dynamic Theory of Organizational Knowledge Creation*
Griselda Pollock's *Vision and Difference*
Amartya Sen's *Inequality Re-Examined*
Susan Sontag's *On Photography*
Yasser Tabbaa's *The Transformation of Islamic Art*
Ludwig von Mises's *Theory of Money and Credit*

Macat Disciplines

Access the greatest ideas and thinkers across entire disciplines, including

THE FUTURE OF DEMOCRACY

Robert A. Dahl's, *Democracy and Its Critics*
Robert A. Dahl's, *Who Governs?*
Alexis De Toqueville's, *Democracy in America*
Niccolò Machiavelli's, *The Prince*
John Stuart Mill's, *On Liberty*
Robert D. Putnam's, *Bowling Alone*
Jean-Jacques Rousseau's, *The Social Contract*
Henry David Thoreau's, *Civil Disobedience*

Macat Disciplines

Access the greatest ideas and thinkers across entire disciplines, including

TOTALITARIANISM

Sheila Fitzpatrick's, *Everyday Stalinism*
Ian Kershaw's, *The "Hitler Myth"*
Timothy Snyder's, *Bloodlands*

Macat Pairs

Analyse historical and modern issues from opposite sides of an argument. Pairs include:

RACE AND IDENTITY

Zora Neale Hurston's
Characteristics of Negro Expression

Using material collected on anthropological expeditions to the South, Zora Neale Hurston explains how expression in African American culture in the early twentieth century departs from the art of white America. At the time, African American art was often criticized for copying white culture. For Hurston, this criticism misunderstood how art works. European tradition views art as something fixed. But Hurston describes a creative process that is alive, ever-changing, and largely improvisational. She maintains that African American art works through a process called 'mimicry'—where an imitated object or verbal pattern, for example, is reshaped and altered until it becomes something new, novel—and worthy of attention.

Frantz Fanon's
Black Skin, White Masks

Black Skin, White Masks offers a radical analysis of the psychological effects of colonization on the colonized.

Fanon witnessed the effects of colonization first hand both in his birthplace, Martinique, and again later in life when he worked as a psychiatrist in another French colony, Algeria. His text is uncompromising in form and argument. He dissects the dehumanizing effects of colonialism, arguing that it destroys the native sense of identity, forcing people to adapt to an alien set of values—including a core belief that they are inferior. This results in deep psychological trauma.

Fanon's work played a pivotal role in the civil rights movements of the 1960s.

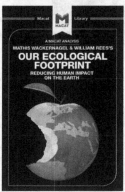

Macat Pairs

*Analyse historical and modern issues
from opposite sides of an argument.
Pairs include:*

Steven Pinker's
The Better Angels of Our Nature

Stephen Pinker's gloriously optimistic 2011 book argues that, despite humanity's biological tendency toward violence, we are, in fact, less violent today than ever before. To prove his case, Pinker lays out pages of detailed statistical evidence. For him, much of the credit for the decline goes to the eighteenth-century Enlightenment movement, whose ideas of liberty, tolerance, and respect for the value of human life filtered down through society and affected how people thought. That psychological change led to behavioral change—and overall we became more peaceful. Critics countered that humanity could never overcome the biological urge toward violence; others argued that Pinker's statistics were flawed.

Philip Zimbardo's
The Lucifer Effect

Some psychologists believe those who commit cruelty are innately evil. Zimbardo disagrees. In *The Lucifer Effect*, he argues that sometimes good people do evil things simply because of the situations they find themselves in, citing many historical examples to illustrate his point. Zimbardo details his 1971 Stanford prison experiment, where ordinary volunteers playing guards in a mock prison rapidly became abusive. But he also describes the tortures committed by US army personnel in Iraq's Abu Ghraib prison in 2003—and how he himself testified in defence of one of those guards. committed by US army personnel in Iraq's Abu Ghraib prison in 2003—and how he himself testified in defence of one of those guards.

Macat Pairs

Analyse historical and modern issues from opposite sides of an argument. Pairs include:

HOW WE RELATE TO EACH OTHER AND SOCIETY

Jean-Jacques Rousseau's
The Social Contract

Rousseau's famous work sets out the radical concept of the 'social contract': a give-and-take relationship between individual freedom and social order.

If people are free to do as they like, governed only by their own sense of justice, they are also vulnerable to chaos and violence. To avoid this, Rousseau proposes, they should agree to give up some freedom to benefit from the protection of social and political organization. But this deal is only just if societies are led by the collective needs and desires of the people, and able to control the private interests of individuals. For Rousseau, the only legitimate form of government is rule by the people.

Robert D. Putnam's
Bowling Alone

In *Bowling Alone*, Robert Putnam argues that Americans have become disconnected from one another and from the institutions of their common life, and investigates the consequences of this change.

Looking at a range of indicators, from membership in formal organizations to the number of invitations being extended to informal dinner parties, Putnam demonstrates that Americans are interacting less and creating less "social capital" – with potentially disastrous implications for their society.

It would be difficult to overstate the impact of *Bowling Alone*, one of the most frequently cited social science publications of the last half-century.

Printed in the United States
by Baker & Taylor Publisher Services

Printed in the United States
by Baker & Taylor Publisher Services